HOW TO
QUILT

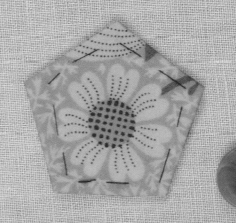

HOW TO
QUILT

TECHNIQUES AND PROJECTS
FOR THE COMPLETE BEGINNER

RACHEL CLARE REYNOLDS

THE GUILD OF MASTER CRAFTSMAN
PUBLICATIONS

First published 2014 by
Guild of Master Craftsman Publications Ltd
Castle Place, 166 High Street, Lewes,
East Sussex BN7 1XU

Text, designs and templates © Rachel Clare Reynolds, 2014
Copyright in the Work © GMC Publications Ltd, 2014

ISBN 978 1 86108 942 7

The publishers and author can accept no legal responsibility for any consequences arising from the application of information, advice or instructions given in this publication.

A catalogue record for this book is available from the British Library.

PUBLISHER Jonathan Bailey
PRODUCTION MANAGER Jim Bulley
MANAGING EDITOR Gerrie Purcell
SENIOR PROJECT EDITOR Dominique Page
EDITOR Robin Pridy
MANAGING ART EDITOR Gilda Pacitti
ART EDITOR Rebecca Mothersole
ILLUSTRATORS Sarah Skeate and Michelle Tilly
PHOTOGRAPHERS Sarah Cuttle and Rebecca Mothersole

Colour origination by GMC Reprographics
Printed and bound in China

CONTENTS

INTRODUCTION

Many people start quilting because they want to make a special quilt for themselves or for their family, then they make another, and so an obsession begins!

A quilt does make a perfect handmade gift but it is not just about the giving. Making anything takes time, and nowadays fashion is transitory, so spending time making a trendy outfit is risky, as by the time you've finished it may no longer be trendy. Time spent making a quilt is never wasted, as it will last a lifetime, giving pleasure long after the outfit would be forgotten.

A quilt can even tell a story. Scraps of material from worn-out clothes or special fabrics, such as an outgrown child's party dress, can be incorporated into a quilt and years later prompt memories of special days. We had a patchwork quilt at home which my mum had made soon after she got married. One of the fabrics was from the dress she was wearing when she first set eyes on my dad. We all thought this was terribly romantic!

Quilting is a great way to learn to sew, even if you are an absolute beginner, as most of the time you will be sewing in a straight line, using easy-to-sew fabrics. Each stitch and technique in this book is carefully explained, step by step, with illustrations. I have tweaked a few of the more difficult aspects to make it even easier and there is even a guide to help you choose fabrics. So, with only the most basic tools and equipment, you can begin to quilt.

Part One will introduce you to the most fundamental stitches and techniques and Part Two introduces ten more techniques and projects, arranged sequentially, starting with the simplest and getting more advanced as you progress through the book. The later projects use a variety of the techniques introduced earlier in the book, guiding you until you are ready to go it alone. For example, Technique Five introduces you to a basic quilt block which can then be used to make the beautiful bed cover at the end of the book.

I do hope this book will entice you into exploring the craft of quilting further. But be warned, quilting can be a seriously addictive pastime.

BEFORE
YOU START

BASIC TOOLS AND EQUIPMENT

ESSENTIAL ITEMS

You don't need specialist quilting tools to start out. In fact, all the projects and techniques in this book use just these items – many you will already have.

1 SCISSORS

You will need a pair of **dressmaking scissors** (A) for cutting fabric; a pair of **paper scissors** (B) for cutting out paper patterns; and small **needlework scissors** (C) for snipping ends of threads.

2 SEAM RIPPER (D)

This is a small tool with a hook on the end. The inside of the hook is sharp and will cut through stitches without cutting fabric.

3 SEWING MACHINE NEEDLES

Using the correct needle is vital when machine sewing – the wrong one can cause thread to bunch or stitches to skip. There are two types needed for the different stages of quilting:

Universal needles (E) are designed for general-purpose sewing when constructing your quilt top. Size 90/14 is a good size for patchworking.

Quilting needles (F) have a slimmer, tapered point and a strong shank to get through layers without skipping stitches. A size 90/14 will cope with most projects.

4 HAND-STITCH NEEDLES

These are numbered 1 to 10, with 1 being the longest and thickest and 10 being the smallest and finest. Here are the basic needles required:

Sharps (G) are used for most forms of hand sewing. They are medium-length with a small round eye and are very sharp.

Quilting needles (H) are sometimes known as Betweens. They are shorter and thinner than Sharps but also have a small round eye and are very sharp. Used for small detailed stitches, they pass through multiple layers easily.

Embroidery needles (I), also known as Crewel needles, have a much larger eye in order to accommodate thicker thread.

5 QUILTING PINS (J)

Thinner and longer than dressmaking pins (K) (although they would be fine), these make it easier to pin multiple layers together. They have a glass head or a large flat head.

6 SAFETY PINS (L)

Used to secure the quilt top, batting and backing fabric together whilst quilting.

7 THIMBLE (M)

For hand sewing – these push the needle through the fabric and protect fingers.

8 MARKERS

You need a **pencil** (N) and **black marker** (O) for marking out measurements and tracing designs, an **air-fade pen** (P) for marking on projects you won't wash and a **light-coloured crayon** (Q) for marking on dark fabrics (check it washes out first).

9 TAPE MEASURE (R)

For accuracy, choose one with both imperial and metric measurements.

10 STEEL RULER (S)

For cutting templates and pattern pieces with a craft knife.

11 CRAFT KNIFE (T)

Recommended to cut out your templates, as it is more accurate than scissors.

12 CUTTING MAT

For cutting with a craft knife. Mats have printed grid lines, which makes cutting squares and rectangles easier.

13 IRONING EQUIPMENT

A good steam iron is essential for pressing seams as well as smoothing out and shaping the fabric. Make sure you have a clean ironing board and cover so you don't transfer any marks to your project.

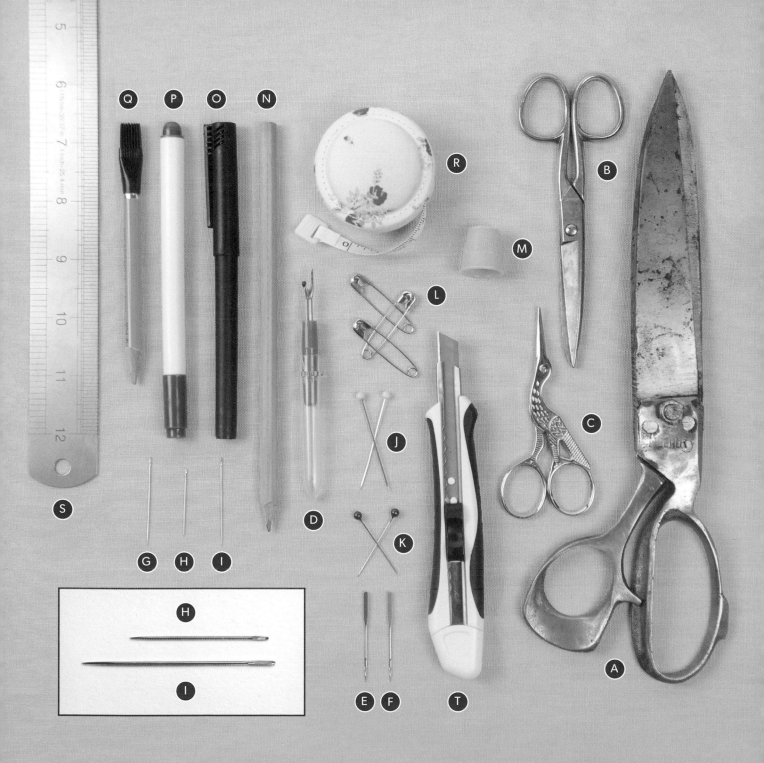

MATERIALS

TYPES OF FABRIC

Although there are many synthetic and natural fabrics, quilting is usually worked in cottons and linens. Linens come in less variety but will create rustic, hardwearing quilts. Beginners should aim to use 100% cotton or linen, as they are the easiest to work with. Most fabric shops have a full section with hundreds of different cotton prints designed specifically for quilting and patchwork and this choice is further extended through the many online stores.

Before you choose a fabric, consider whether it is pre-shrunk. If not pre-shrunk, or washed before sewing, then each fabric layer may shrink a bit the first time the quilt is washed. If this happens, the quilt will have tiny puckers across the surface caused by the different layers pulling against each other. Some people love this look, while some prefer to keep the quilt top smooth so always wash their fabric before they start their project. I think puckering adds to the character of the quilt, so I don't check for pre-shrunk fabric or wash it before I start.

Tip Keep to the same type of fabric within a project. You'll need the fabrics to behave in the same way, both while sewing and when washing the finished project afterwards.

COLOUR AND PATTERN

Fabrics that are good for quilting and patchworking can be sorted according to colour and pattern. It is important to mix colours up and to use a variety of large and small prints along with some plain fabrics within a project to create a balanced look.

Choosing fabric for quilting might seem simple, a matter of picking all your favourite fabrics and mixing them up. Unfortunately, it is not so easy, and the huge variety can be overwhelming. But it is important to get the choice right, as there is nothing more disheartening then investing time and money creating a quilted masterpiece, only to realize you made a mistake with your choice of fabrics.

Often fabrics come as part of a range of prints that are designed to go together. If you find the process of choosing by yourself too daunting then these ranges are sold in pre-selected packs, with the fabric either cut as fat quarters, 18 x 22in (46 x 56cm) squares of fabric, or they are sold as Jelly Rolls, rolls of 30, 2½in (6cm) strips.

Don't be afraid to seek help – shop assistants will be happy to advise.

You can buy complementary strips of fabric as a Jelly Roll (left) or squares of fabric as fat quarters (below).

BASIC RULES FOR PATCHWORK

For a patchwork quilt top with many different fabrics, it is best to stick to a colour scheme and use a variety of prints that work together. Following this set of rules will take out the guesswork.

- Find a fabric you like that has a large print and contains at least five colours **A**; this fabric will anchor all the others together.

- Study the print and pick out its colours. There will be a series of dots along the fabric edge, one of each of the printed colours, which helps to isolate the colours.

- Find two fabrics in those chosen colours, each with a small print **B** & **C**. If the fabrics have a background colour, make sure it is the same throughout your fabrics; beige, grey or white work well.

- Choose two plain fabrics, in colours picked from the first fabric **D** & **E**. Aim for one light and one darker fabric. They needn't be exactly the same shade; a variety can add interest.

- You now have the five fabrics that will form your quilt's basic structure. Add between three and five more fabrics **F**, **G**, **H**, **I** & **J**, depending on the project you are working on. Be guided by the following points:

- Aim for equal amounts of small prints, large prints, plains and each of your chosen colours.

- Be sure to balance the light and dark, aiming for equality: if you have nine fabrics, try to include three light, three medium and three darker fabrics. Spread these across the chosen colours and prints, which will mean: don't have all of your larger prints in darker shades and all the smaller prints in light colours.

- Step back and stare. Does one stand out too much? Do you like them? Is one your favourite, but it doesn't go with the rest? Too much of one colour? Is the background colour the same throughout? Swap fabrics that are not working. Once you have gained confidence in your ability to successfully match fabrics, you can start to experiment and break the basic rules. When this happens, you will know that you are a quilter.

THREAD

When constructing your quilt top it is best to use a neutral thread to match all the different prints you are using for your project. Then at the quilting stage, when securing the three layers together, you may wish to use a contrasting thread that will emphasize the quilting pattern.

④ General-purpose thread

When sewing on the machine or by hand, a cotton general-purpose, or standard, thread is best for quilting, as it is stronger than polyester, which can stretch a bit.

BATTING/WADDING

This is the padding in a quilt. Batting is the term most commonly used for cotton while wadding is used for polyester. It can also come in wool.

⑤ Quilting thread

A wider variety of thread is used when hand quilting. The intricate patterns that experts stitch across the whole quilt are generally worked in quilting thread, which is thicker than general-purpose thread and slightly hairy so it grips the fabric.

① Cotton

Thin but warm and hardwearing, cotton drapes well and washes easily.

② Polyester

Generally thicker than cotton and much lighter, polyester is good to use for a child's quilt. It also washes well and is easy to use. I favour cotton batting for most of my projects, as I prefer natural fibres, but I will use polyester for an extra squidgy look.

⑥ Embroidery perle thread

This is a thicker cotton thread, used for embroidery, but which is also good for hand-tied and simple hand quilting. It has a slight sheen and comes in many colours.

③ Wool

Less commonly used, as it is more expensive, but beautifully warm and some quilters feel it gives a better finish.

⑦ No. 8 or 10 cotton crochet thread

Also used for hand quilting, this thicker thread helps to emphasize the stitches more. It comes in a wide variety of colours and is great for the beginner quilter, as it is easier to use and quick to stitch with.

OTHER MATERIALS

8 **Iron-on transfer adhesive**
Commonly known as Bondaweb (or WonderUnder in the US), this has a fine layer of adhesive on one side to adhere two pieces of fabric together (see Table Runner, page 102).

9 **Tracing/parchment paper**
Used to transfer designs and templates onto fabric. No special type is needed and greaseproof or parchment paper from the kitchen will do nicely (see Cushion, page 94).

10 **Buttons**
Attractive buttons are very useful as embellishments. Self-covered buttons come in two halves and a small piece of fabric is used to cover them so they match the project being worked on (see Pinboard, page 76).

11 **Stuffing**
Usually made from polyester, but you can also buy woollen stuffing (see Lavender Keepsake, page 36).

12 **Upholstery webbing**
This makes great strapping and handles for bags (see Duffel Bag, page 58).

SEWING BASICS

FOLLOWING THE INSTRUCTIONS

The most frequent phrase in sewing instructions is 'place fabric right sides together'. This must always be followed if you want all your stitches and seams to end up in the right place. The reason behind the instruction is that most stitching is done on the wrong side of the fabric. This way, when the project is finished, all the stitching ends up hidden on the inside. It is very important to follow the instructions in this regard. Throughout the techniques and projects, the following abbreviations are used:

RST   Right Sides Together
RSD   Right Side Down
RSU   Right Side Up
WST   Wrong Sides Together
WSU   Wrong Side Up
WSD   Wrong Side Down

When looking at the illustrations, the following colours are used:

Right side of fabric

Wrong side of fabric

Right side of backing fabric or lining

Wrong side of backing fabric or lining

Batting or wadding

Other materials

SEAM ALLOWANCES

When cutting out fabric, it is important to have enough extra fabric to sew the seams without making your project too small. To ensure this, a small amount of fabric called the seam allowance is included around the actual size wanted. How much extra depends on the task in hand, but for quilting, it is traditionally ¼in (6mm). It can be tricky for a novice to accurately sew so close to the edge of the fabric; therefore, throughout most of this book, I have increased the seam allowance to ½in (12mm), which allows for a greater margin of error. This amount is far easier to work with and it allows for a wobble here and there. With more experience, you may want to use the standard seam allowance, for less wastage and a less bulky quilt. In metric, 12mm may seem an awkward measurement. You can increase this to 15mm, but remember to be consistent and stick to the same seam allowance throughout a project.

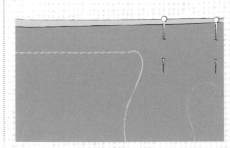

A WORD ABOUT MEASUREMENTS...

Make sure you use either the metric or the imperial measurements. Do not mix measurements, as the conversions are not exact and your quilt may not end up the size you expected.

IRONING

It is important to iron all your fabrics before you start a project. This may seem like an extra and unnecessary chore, but it is far easier to work with wrinkle-free fabric. It is also far easier to iron a large piece of fabric than lots of little pieces. It is especially important to iron your quilt top, batting and backing fabric before you start to quilt them, as once quilted it is very hard to iron them properly.

While constructing your quilt top, you will often be instructed to iron your seams in various different directions; this is so the next set of seams to be sewn will fit together well. At times, this may get confusing but if the odd set of seams are facing the wrong way, don't worry – they will not show on the finished quilt!

When ironing small pieces of fabric, try to press down, rather than moving the iron across the surface as this can distort the shape of the blocks.

A seam ironed flat. This one faces upwards, but sometimes you will need to iron them facing down.

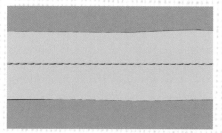

A seam ironed open. Often the last seam on a quilt top will need to be pressed open.

PINNING AND TACKING

How you pin your work together will again depend on the project you are working on. The basic function of pins is to temporarily hold pieces of fabric together until they are secured by stitching. Traditionally, the layers are first pinned together, then tacked and finally sewn together, either by hand or machine.

Many sewers and quilters now forego the tacking stage and move straight from pins to stitch, which saves vast amounts of time. Tacking is still an important step when quilting the quilt top, batting and backing fabric together but I must confess, apart from this step, I stopped tacking as soon as my needlework teacher stopped looking over my shoulder.

PIN FOR HAND STITCH

Place your pins parallel to the seam or hem you are stitching. Remove the pins as you get to them.

PIN FOR MACHINE STITCH

Place your pins perpendicular to the seam or hem you are stitching, removing them as you go. Try not to stitch over the pins with the machine, as this can break the needle or damage the machine.

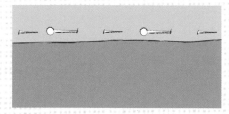

Pinning for hand stitch

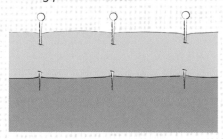

Pinning for machine stitch

HAND STITCH BASICS

STARTING AND FINISHING

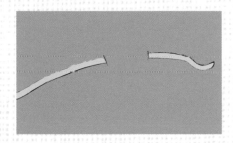 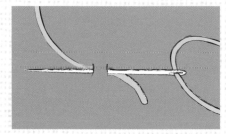 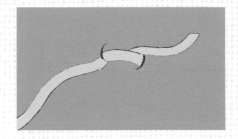

1 Always use approximately 20in (50cm) of thread when hand sewing, unless tacking. If you use more thread it will tangle. Start with the wrong side of the fabric facing you and take one small stitch. Pull the thread through but leave a short tail.

2 Take one or two more stitches over the top of the first stitch and pull tight. Alternatively, to start stitching, you may prefer to tie a small knot in the end of the thread and hide the knot in the seam or the back of the fabric.

3 To finish stitching (this is sometimes called casting off) take one or two more stitches over the top of the last stitch and pull tight to secure the thread.

RUNNING, TACKING AND QUILTING STITCHES

These three are the same basic stitch. Pass the needle in and out of the fabric, making the top stitches equal in length. The length of the stitches on the underside should also be of equal length but may be shorter than the top stitch.

Running stitch is the most basic of stitches. Tacking (or basting) stitches are longer and used to temporarily secure layers of fabric together before sewing. Quilting stitches are tiny running stitches, used to secure the three layers of a quilt together.

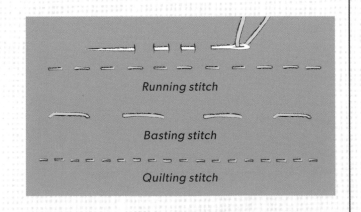

Running stitch

Basting stitch

Quilting stitch

WHIP STITCH

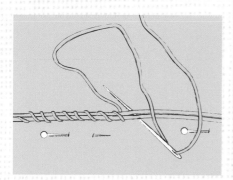

This stitch – also known as overcast stitch or oversew stitch – is used to join two edges of fabric together, and is useful for closing gaps. Fold over any raw edges and pin together so the edges of the fabric are parallel. Starting at the left (or right if you are left-handed) and working towards the right, push the needle through the fabric, from front to back, about 1/16in (1.5mm) from the folded edge of the fabric. Slant your needle so it comes out slightly behind itself, then pull tight and repeat.

Tip Most hand stitches are worked from right to left, as shown throughout the book. If you are left-handed, you may need to work in the other direction.

HEMMING STITCH

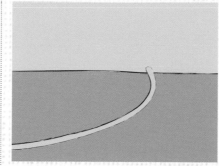

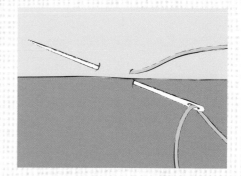

1 There is more than one way to sew a hem and this is the stitch best suited to securing your quilt binding (see page 28 for more on binding). Start by securing your thread inside the hem where it won't show. Bring the thread up through the folded edge of the fabric you are going to hem, about 1/16in (1.5mm) from the edge.

2 Working right to left (reverse if left-handed), take a stitch in the base fabric and start directly under where you have started. Holding the needle at a slight slant, slide through the base fabric and batting and bring the needle back up through the base fabric and the folded edge, 1/4in (6mm) further along.

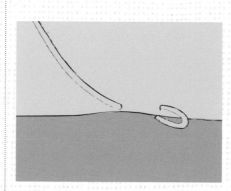

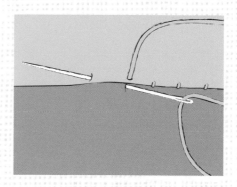

3 Pull your thread tight to form your first stitch. Repeat to form a row of stitching.

4 You will see only tiny stitches on the fabric surface – the rest is hidden inside the quilt, meaning it is less likely to catch and wear over time.

MACHINE STITCH BASICS

People often say to me they would love to be able to sew but don't know how to use a sewing machine. I always recommend they should learn to quilt, as it involves lots of stitching in a straight line and so is a great way to learn how to use a machine.

Every machine is different, so refer to your user manual for instructions. When just starting out, however, you can ignore all the sections in the user manual except the following:

- the first section, which tells you what all the buttons and knobs are for;
- the section on how to thread the machine and wind the bobbin;
- the instructions for straight stitch and reverse stitch;
- and finally, it is very worth your while to get to know the troubleshooting section at the end.

The following basic machine stitch skills are all you will need in order to complete the techniques and projects in this book and I have also included a brief guide to the most common problems that you might encounter.

STARTING AND FINISHING

Place your fabric under the needle and lower the presser foot. Slowly press the foot pedal to start stitching. Sew about ¼in (6mm) then press down the reverse sewing lever and reverse stitch for a few stitches. Release and begin sewing forwards again; this secures the threads. Repeat this process at the end of your stitching to secure threads at both ends.

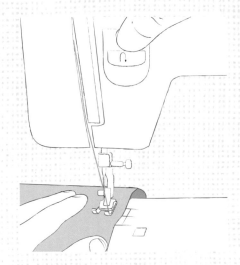

STITCHING IN A STRAIGHT LINE

To machine stitch in a straight line, do not watch the needle. Instead, watch the fabric edge and make sure it always stays the same distance away from the edge of the presser foot. Use your hand to guide the fabric through the machine but do not pull it from behind. Try to keep the bulk of the fabric to the left of the machine.

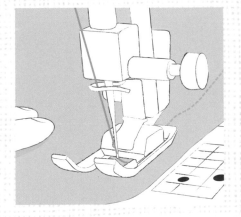

Tip Always check your stitches on a sample of the same fabric you will be using for your project, with the same amount of layers, before you start.

SEAM ALLOWANCE GUIDES

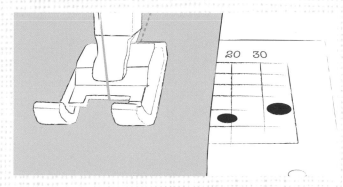

These are engraved onto the sewing machine's base plate, just to the right of the presser foot. Keeping the edge of the fabric running parallel to these guides will allow you to keep to a set seam allowance. To use these guides accurately, your needle must be positioned centrally.

TURNING A CORNER

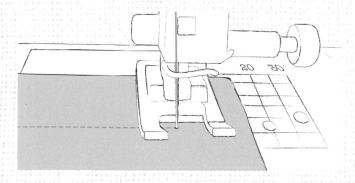

Stop sewing at the point where you wish to turn; exactly where will depend on your seam allowance, but if you are working with a ½in (12mm) seam allowance then this will be ½in (12mm) from the edge. Stop with the needle down through the fabric. Lift the presser foot and swivel the fabric 90 degrees; drop the presser foot and continue.

MACHINE TROUBLESHOOTING

Bottom thread showing on top of fabric
Top thread tension is too tight – loosen slightly using the tension dial.

Top thread showing on bottom of fabric
Top thread tension is too loose – tighten slightly using the tension dial.

Thread bunches on back of fabric
The machine is incorrectly threaded; rethread it while the presser foot is up, take out the bobbin, clean out any fluff and replace. If this doesn't work then the tension may be too loose – tighten it using the tension dial.

Bunching on back of fabric when you start to stitch
Make sure you pull approximately 4in (10cm) of both the upper thread and bobbin thread to the back of the machine and hold as you begin to stitch.

Skipped stitches
This is usually caused by using the wrong needle for the fabric you are sewing, or the needle may be blunt.

Tip If you find it hard to remember which way to turn the dial to loosen or tighten the tension on your sewing machine, remember – 'lefty loosy, righty tighty'!

QUILTING BASICS

WHAT MAKES A QUILT A QUILT?

Quilting simply means to make a warm cover from two layers of fabric with padding in between. The top layer is called the quilt top, the padding is known as batting or wadding and the bottom layer is called the backing fabric. These layers are secured together either by being tied or sewn. The craft of quilting has now grown to include a vast array of different techniques and processes but these three basic layers, which are tied or stitched together, remain constant.

PATCHWORK

One of the most popular techniques associated with quilting and one many people will think of when imagining a traditional quilt is patchworking. This technique developed at a time when recycling was a necessity and people would sew pieces of worn-out clothing together to form quilt tops. Patchwork quilts are built up from smaller units called quilt blocks, which are themselves made by sewing together smaller pieces of fabric.

QUILT BLOCKS

Constructing quilt blocks is explored in Technique Five (see page 64) with instructions to make a simple Nine Patch quilt block and Disappearing Nine Patch, then again in Technique Seven (see page 82) with the London Stairs block. But these are just a couple of the many different quilt block designs to try once the basics have been learnt. Flying Geese, Pinwheel and Snowball are just a few that come to mind.

Although there are many different ways of quilting, there is one thing on which all quilters will agree: accuracy as you work is vital. All your quilt blocks need to be the same size so they can be sewn together with all the seams lined up. This means you need to get into the habit of cutting your pieces all the same size and sewing the seam allowance accurately. The traditional quilter's seam allowance of ¼in (6mm) has been increased to ½in (12mm) in this book to make it easier for the beginner quilter.

There are many methods of quilting; two examples being Hand-tied quilting (far left) and English Paper Piecing (left).

Tip The techniques on the following pages are key elements of the quilting process and you will need to refer back to them while working on the projects in this book.

SQUARING UP

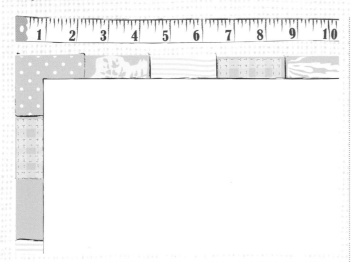

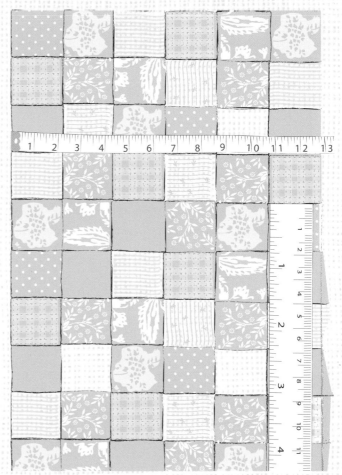

1 Before you construct your quilt top, check that all your quilt blocks are square. Do this either with a tape measure or by checking against a paper template that has been cut to the exact size your block should be. Trim any wonky edges, but do not trim smaller than your template. If only one piece of fabric within the block is slightly short, leave it. But if the whole block is too small, you will have to remake it.

Tip If you are an absolute beginner, start small. Don't go for that double quilt top just yet. Read up on these basics, then try one of this book's smaller projects before trying to recreate one of Granny's quilting masterpieces.

2 After assembling the blocks into the quilt top, check your measurements – top, bottom and also both sides – to make sure it is not wider at the top than the bottom, before going any further. If you need to trim, fold in half and trim both sides together rather than just the one. Trim as little as possible so your blocks do not become distorted.

PREPARING THE QUILT SANDWICH

When the quilt top, batting and backing fabric are put together they are referred to as the 'quilt sandwich'. These layers have to be carefully prepared for quilting.

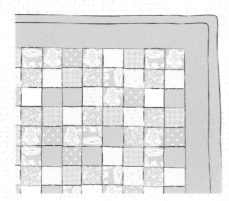 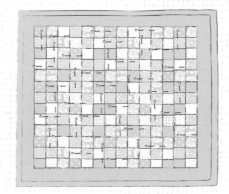 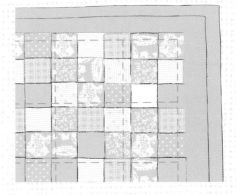

1 First cut out the backing fabric and batting, ensuring they are 3in (7.5cm), larger all round than the quilt top. Iron each layer. Lay the backing fabric RSD on a flat surface, smoothing out any wrinkles. Place your batting on top of this. Again, smooth out any wrinkles, and make sure it is lined up with the backing fabric. Next, place your quilt top RSU, on top of the batting and make sure it is central with the batting and backing fabric.

2 Pin the layers together, starting from the centre and working towards the edges, smoothing wrinkles as you go. Gently tug the backing fabric, without shifting its position, to remove any wrinkles that may be underneath. Try not to lift the sandwich too much as you pin.

3 Finally, tack the layers together. Starting at the centre, work rows of stitching across the shorter sides, about every 4in (10cm) until you reach the outer edge, then tack down the length of the quilt, again in evenly spaced rows. You should end up with a grid pattern. Make sure you tack firmly, so the layers can't shift.

Tip When quilting any project, always start stitching in the middle of the quilt and work towards the edge. It can also be difficult to feed a large quilt through a sewing machine. The trick is to roll most of the fabric. This will then be easier to fit through the machine.

QUILTING LAYERS

Although all quilts are made up of three layers, stitched or tied together, there are many ways this can be done, each of which will result in different effects. These can be loosely separated into three methods: hand-stitched quilting, hand-tied quilting and machine quilting.

In Part Two of this book I introduce one unique technique associated with each of these methods. Hand-tied quilting with embellishments is explained fully on page 48. English Whole Cloth quilting (a traditional hand-stitched quilting technique) is explored on page 90, while a simple machine-stitch quilting technique that allows you to 'draw' with stitches is introduced on page 98.

The rest of the techniques and projects use the following three methods to quilt the layers together: Outline quilting, Parallel Lines and Stitch in the Ditch. These are the techniques most often used when quilting a patchwork top and stitching either by hand or machine, you will need to refer back to these at various points throughout the book.

OUTLINE QUILTING

Usually done by hand, each piece is simply outlined about ¼in (6mm) inside the seam, with quilting stitch (see page 20).

PARALLEL LINES

1 Starting in the middle, divide the quilt sandwich in half with a row of stitches across its width. Run rows of parallel stitches approximately 10in (25cm) apart until you reach the outer edge, then go back to the middle of the quilt and repeat, working towards the other side.

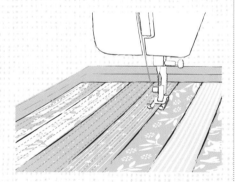

2 Fill in between these rows with parallel lines of stitches to further secure the layers. Lines of stitches can either be regularly spaced or random.

STITCH IN THE DITCH

This is a great way of quilting when you want the quilting stitches to be unobtrusive. Often used to complement a patchwork quilt top, this technique uses rows of stitches placed right in the seam lines. Starting in the middle of the quilt, stitch each of the seams where the pieces are joined. Stitch each seam in turn, working towards the outer edge. Stitch across the quilt first and then lengthways.

BINDING EDGES

The final stage to any quilting project is to finish off the edges, and this is usually done by binding, which creates a solid border around the edge of the quilt and hides the edges of all the layers. Binding is made from strips of fabric that are cut along the grain, usually in the same fabric as the backing fabric. Or, if there are curved edges, sometimes bias binding (strips of fabric cut diagonally across the grain of the fabric) is used, giving it a slight stretch.

The width of the binding strip you need to cut will depend on the project but will be double the final width of your binding plus double your seam allowance. For example, if you want your binding to be 2in (5cm) wide and you are working with a ½in (12mm) seam allowance, then the strip you need to cut will be 5in (12.4cm) (2 + 2 + ½ + ½) wide. To work out the length of binding you need, measure around the quilt and add approximately 12in (30cm). To save fabric, cut across the width of your fabric where possible.

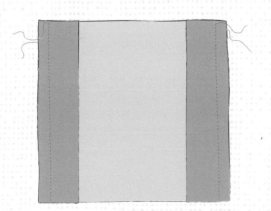

1 Take one strip and place RST alongside one of the edges of your quilt. Pin for machine stitch (see page 19) and then sew. For all the projects in this book, use a ½in (12mm) seam allowance. Repeat this step on the opposite side of the quilt, as shown. Iron the strips open.

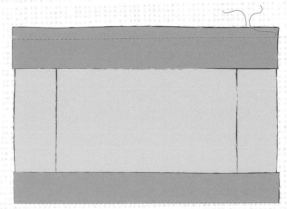

2 Repeat step 1 and attach strips to the other two sides. Double check your first two strips are opened out before you start. Pin and then sew right across these first two binding strips. Trim strips so they are level with the first strips and then iron all strips open.

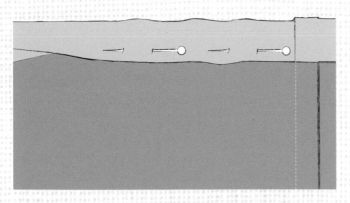

Tip Always fold over and pin two opposite sides first.

3 Flip the quilt over, folding the edge of the binding over by the seam allowance you are working with. Fold again and pin just below the line of stitching. On large projects, it is best to start in the middle of one side and work towards each end.

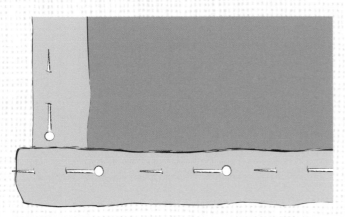

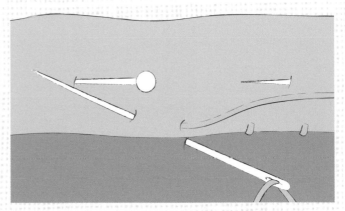

4 Repeat step 3 along the remaining sides. When you get to the corners, try to ensure the fold stays consistent.

5 Use hemming stitch (see page 21) to secure the binding. Iron when complete.

TECHNIQUES
& PROJECTS

ENGLISH PAPER PIECING

THIS IS THE PERFECT PLACE TO START YOUR QUILTING JOURNEY. YOU ONLY NEED TO LEARN A COUPLE OF SIMPLE HAND STITCHES FOR THIS EASY TECHNIQUE, WHICH CAN THEN BE USED TO BUILD UP AN ARRAY OF INTRICATE PATCHWORK PATTERNS.

English Paper Piecing is one of the most traditional techniques of constructing a patchwork quilt top. Originating in England, where people would use scraps of worn-out clothes for the material, it has grown from its humble beginnings into an amazing art form that quilters all over the world enjoy.

The term 'piecing' simply means sewing pieces of fabric together to form a larger section of fabric, and 'paper piecing' involves the use of paper templates. These templates are cut to the exact size you want the finished patch. Fabric is then tacked around each paper shape and, leaving the paper attached to the fabric, all the pieces are then sewn together, avoiding the paper template so it can be removed later.

The patterns created rely on simple geometry: the patches must tessellate, or fit together, without any gaps. By following this basic rule, you can develop a nearly infinite variety of patterns, with the choice of fabric dictating the overall effect.

This is a good technique for the beginner to learn because the paper templates stay tacked onto the fabric until after the work is complete. This means the fabric does not move around or stretch out of shape, and the all-important seam allowance is tacked firmly in place so it can't give the quilter any problems. The construction technique is the same, whatever the actual shape of your paper pieces, but their shape will determine the pattern that is created and whether the pieces come together to form a three-dimensional form or a flat surface.

To demonstrate the technique, I have used hexagonal papers to create one of the most well-known patterns, which is sometimes referred to as Grandmother's Flower Garden.

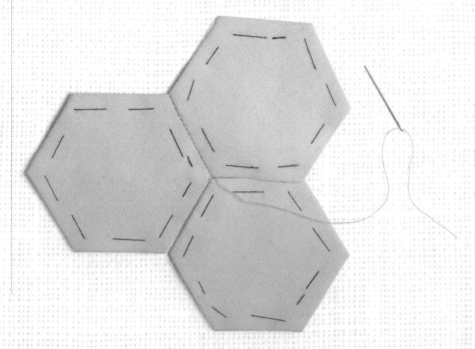

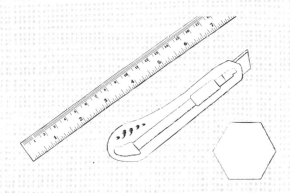

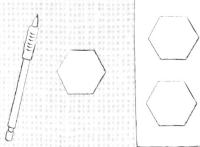

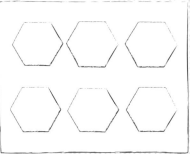

1 First, you need to create a template of your shape. Be as accurate as you can, as this template will be used to cut out all of your paper pieces. Cut your template from medium-thickness card. Always use a craft knife and a steel ruler if you can, as they are more accurate than scissors. Mark your template 'Master'.

2 Take some thin card or thick paper and draw around your template. Draw as many shapes, in this case, hexagons, as you need, then cut them out. Be consistent; always cut inside the line or always outside, not a mixture of both.

Tip Cutting the paper pieces can be a boring and laborious process. It is possible to buy pre-cut paper pieces or, to save making a template and drawing each piece by hand, you can use a computer. Simply copy and paste your shape onto a page, fitting in as many as possible without them touching. Then print out onto thin card.

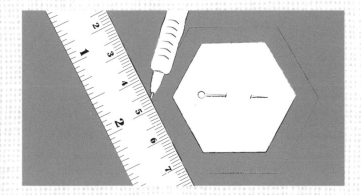

3 Pin one of the papers onto your chosen fabric. Remember, this paper piece is the exact size of the finished patch. Mark a ⅜in (10mm) seam allowance around the paper with a pencil. With experience, this seam allowance can be reduced to ¼in (6mm) in order to save fabric but, for now, leave a larger amount. Cut as many pieces as you need.

Tip With experience you will find that you do not need to mark the seam allowance with a pencil before cutting your fabric. Simply estimate the seam allowance and cut by eye.

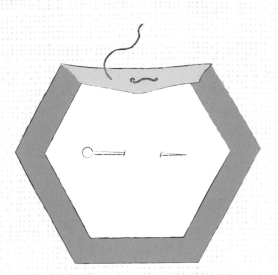

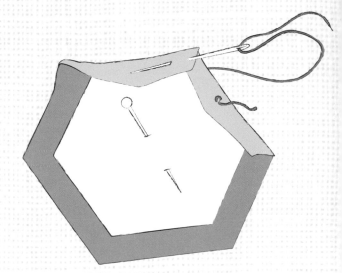

4 Take one of your pieces and fold the fabric over one straight edge of the paper. The fabric should be tight up against the paper but the paper should not be folded. Crease the fabric along this fold with your fingers. Starting in the centre of this side, make one tacking stitch (see page 20).

5 Before you take the next stitch, fold the fabric over the next straight side and crease. Now take the next stitch, securing all folded fabric at the corner. Take one stitch along the second side, then fold over the third side before stitching through this corner.

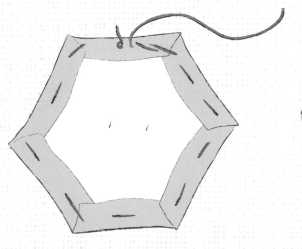

6 Keep going until all the sides are secure. Repeat with all the fabric patches.

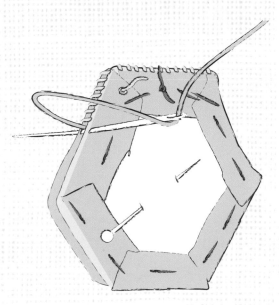

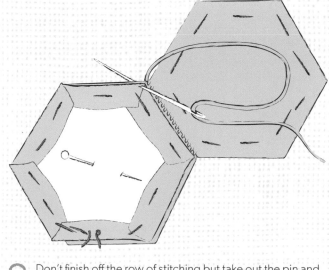

7 Place two of your patches RST, ensuring the corners of each shape line up. Pin them together in the middle. Starting in one corner, whip stitch (see page 21) along one side, avoiding the paper template. I do a double stitch at the beginning of the side and one at the end, to make it strong.

8 Don't finish off the row of stitching but take out the pin and open out the shapes. Take another fabric patch and pin, RST, to one of the two already sewn together. Continue to whip stitch along the adjoining edge.

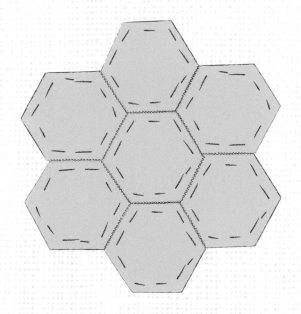

9 Continue pinning and whip stitching more pieces together. Sometimes it will be possible to sew more than one side without finishing a stitch but often only one side at a time can be sewn.

LAVENDER KEEPSAKE

MAKE A SOPHISTICATED LAVENDER-FILLED VERSION OF THE CLASSIC PATCHWORK BALL
TO LIGHTLY SCENT YOUR WARDROBE OR DRAWERS. THESE PRETTY BEDROOM ADORNMENTS
ARE QUICK AND EASY TO SEW AND MAKE THE IDEAL HOMEMADE GIFT.

YOU WILL NEED

- A variety of six cotton fabrics of the same weight, in 5in (13cm) squares
- A handful of stuffing
- 4in (10cm) satin ribbon or yarn
- Matching general-purpose thread
- Dressmaking, paper and small needlework scissors
- A No.9 sharp or embroidery needle
- Quilting or dressmaking pins
- Thimble
- Seam ripper
- Craft knife, steel ruler and cutting mat
- Pencil
- Medium-thickness card
- Thin card
- Dried lavender flowers
- Template on page 114

FINISHED SIZE

3in (8cm) in diameter

TECHNIQUES USED

English Paper Piecing (see page 32)

Tacking stitch (see page 20)

Whip stitch (see page 21)

Pin for hand stitch (see page 19)

MATERIALS TO USE

To avoid two of the same pieces being side by side, use at least six different fabrics (see pages 14–15 for a guide to choosing fabric). Many shops will sell as little as 4in (10cm), or you can use scraps from favourite old clothes or covers.

Tip

Use nursery fabrics and enlarge the pentagon template to approximately 3in (8cm) across to turn this into a child's play ball. Slip in a couple of bells with the stuffing for added play value.

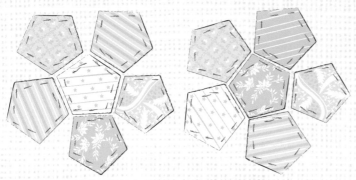 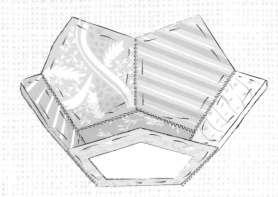

1 Follow the instructions for English Paper Piecing to make 12 pentagon patches using the template provided. Arrange these as two 'flowers', rearranging your different fabrics until you are happy. Try to avoid having the same patterns or colours next to each other.

2 Using whip stitch, and referring back to the English Paper Piecing instructions, sew your first 'flower' into a bowl. The pentagons will naturally pull the sides of the bowl upwards. The inside of the bowl is the right side of the fabric.

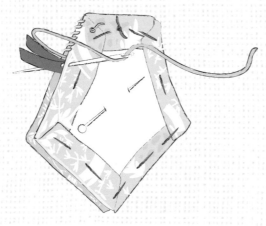 

3 If you want your ball to have a loop to hang it up with, add this while you are constructing the second bowl. Take a length of ribbon about 4in (10cm) long and fold it in half. Sandwich it between two pentagons just before you sew them, with the ends of the ribbon poking through the top edge. Sew through the ribbon as you sew the two pentagons together.

Tip These keepsakes also make great Christmas tree decorations if constructed in festive fabrics. Cinnamon bark could be used instead of lavender for a delicious scent.

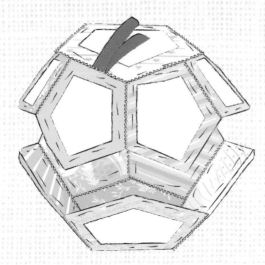

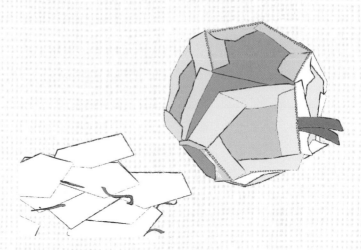

4 Sew the bowls together. Each will have a zig-zagged 'top' to slot together – points going into hollows. Keeping one of the points lined up with one of the hollows, slide the bowls slightly so that the straight edges come together and can be pinned and whip stitched. Once the first edge is sewn, continue joining the two bowls together, matching the corners up as you go. Leave the last two sides open.

5 Cut and remove the tacking stitches and remove all the papers. Turn the ball the right way out. Do this by putting your fingers through the hole and pulling the inside slowly up through the hole. Be careful not to strain the stitching.

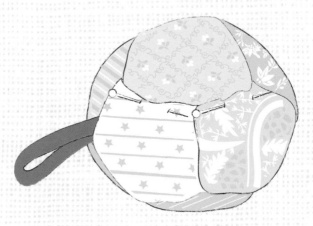

6 Fill your ball by feeding a small amount of stuffing into the ball at a time so that it pads out evenly. Make a hollow in the middle of the stuffing and pour in a couple of spoonfuls or sprigs of dried lavender and then add more stuffing.

7 To sew up the opening, first pin the two open sides and use whip stitch to secure them together. You may find you need to poke in a little bit more stuffing just before you close the hole completely.

Lavender keepsake

RAG QUILTING

THIS VERSATILE TECHNIQUE WILL GIVE YOU PLENTY OF PRACTICE IN BASIC MACHINE SKILLS BEFORE MOVING ONTO MORE COMPLEX QUILTING PROJECTS. IT IS QUICK, SIMPLE AND THE RESULTS ARE DECEPTIVELY IMPRESSIVE.

A Rag quilt is not, as the name implies, made from rags but rather has ragged seams. When sewing, the raw edges of the fabric are usually covered or hemmed; with Rag quilting, the seams are left exposed and allowed to fray, becoming a striking feature of the quilt.

This technique is ideal for a beginner because each piece or square is quilted individually and then sewn together – meaning there are no large pieces of backing fabric or batting to worry about. After you have cut out your fabric pieces, all that is needed is the ability to sew in a straight line! And don't worry if even your straight lines are a bit wobbly at first – the wobbles won't show, and by the time you have finished your first quilt you will be able to sew straight lines with your eyes shut.

Like all patchwork techniques, Rag quilting is very versatile and the fabric you choose will influence the finished article, so think carefully about colour and pattern before you start to sew (see pages 14–15 for advice on choosing your fabrics). Sizes of the finished pieces can vary, but are usually squares between 6in (15cm) and 8½in (22cm). How many pieces you have will depend on how big you want your finished quilt, but it is amazing how quickly this technique builds up. The only rule is that the fabric must be able to fray so you get the lovely soft seams between each piece.

1 Using your own paper templates, cut out your pieces of fabric and batting. Their size and quantity will depend on the project you are working on, but always cut the batting piece 1½in (4cm) smaller than the fabric piece to allow for the ragged seams.

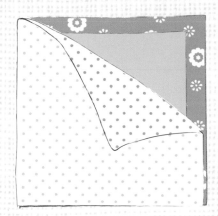

2 Assemble your mini-quilt sandwiches (see page 26), taking two pieces of fabric and one piece of batting. Place the batting, centrally, in between the two pieces of fabric. Pin in place.

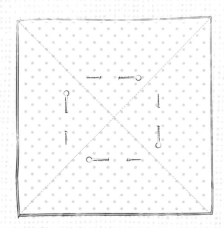

3 Machine sew diagonally from corner to corner across each of the sandwiches to form a cross securing the batting.

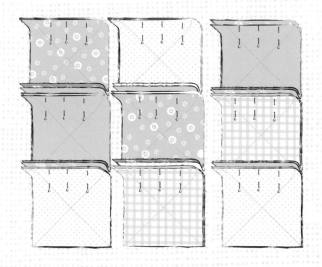

4 Pin the sandwiches together for machine stitch (see page 19), forming strips. Make sure all seams face the same way.

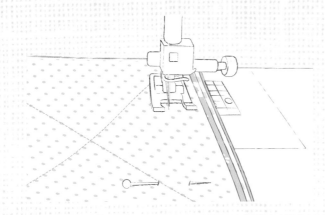

5 Sew the sandwiches together to form strips, using a seam allowance of ¾in (2cm). Use the guide on your machine to keep the seam straight (see page 23). Try to sew right up next to the batting inside each sandwich. Reverse stitch at the beginning and end of stitching (see page 22).

Tip Most rag quilts are made up from rows of squares – although there is no reason why you cannot use rectangles or long strips instead. Once you know the basics, don't be afraid to experiment.

6 Pin the first two strips together, placing one on top of the other with the seams facing outwards and with the pieces neatly in line with each other. Position as shown, with one seam pushed flat one way and the other side pushed the other way. Pin through all the layers of both seams, so they don't move while you are sewing.

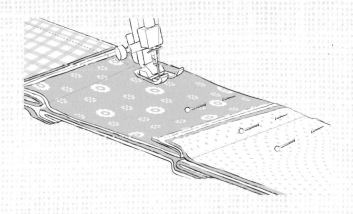

Tip It may be very tempting to throw the whole quilt in the washing machine to start the fraying process off, but Rag quilting creates so many loose threads that you may block the filter of your machine if you do this. It is far better to wash it in the bath first by hand, before risking your machine.

7 Sew the strips together – again, use a ¾in (2cm) seam allowance. Sew the strips so you are stitching towards the flap of the top seam; this helps prevent the bottom seam from snagging on the machine foot. Pin the next strip to the two already joined and sew.

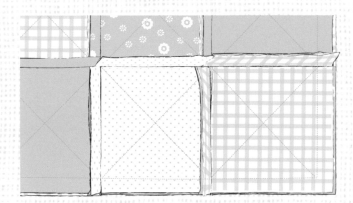

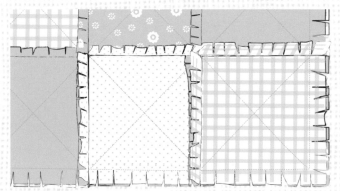

8 How many strips you sew together depends on the project but when complete, trim the edges of the quilt so everything is straight and then sew right around the quilt, ¾in (2cm) in from the edge.

9 To help start the fraying process, snip the seams (being careful not to snip through your stitches) every 1in (25mm). The last thing to do is to take your finished quilt outside and give it a good brush and a shake. All the loose threads will start to come off the seams and you will have the beginnings of your 'rag' effect. Wash by hand.

THROW

THIS QUILTED THROW WILL SOON BECOME INDISPENSABLE FOR ALL SEASONS, FROM SNUGGLING DOWN ON COLD WINTER NIGHTS IN FRONT OF A FIRE TO ENJOYING SUMMER PICNICS ON THE BEACH. IT IS VERY ROBUST. IN FACT, THE MORE YOU WASH IT, THE BETTER IT LOOKS.

YOU WILL NEED

- Four 34 x 59in (88 x 150cm) pieces of contrasting 100% brushed cotton fabrics
- 31in (80cm) of cotton batting, 90in (228cm) wide
- Contrasting general-purpose machine thread
- Dressmaking, paper and small needlework scissors
- Machine quilting needle (size 90/14)
- Quilting or dressmaking pins
- Thimble
- Seam ripper
- Tape measure
- Craft knife, steel ruler and cutting mat
- Pencil, paper and marker pen
- One 8½in (22cm) and one 7in (18cm) square paper template made from thin card

FINISHED SIZE

42 x 56in (108 x 144cm)

TECHNIQUES USED

Rag quilting (see page 40)
Stitching in a straight line (see page 22)
Turning a corner (see page 23)
Seam allowance guides (see page 23)

MATERIALS TO USE

The amounts given are the exact amounts needed for this project but it's always a good idea to buy a little extra fabric, just in case. For a thicker yet lighter throw, choose polyester wadding rather than cotton batting.

Tip

To quickly and accurately cut your squares of fabric, cut strips across the width of your fabric. Then, using your template as a guide, cut these strips into squares. To speed things up you can cut two layers of fabric at once.

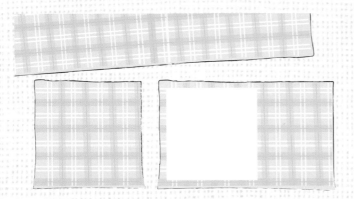

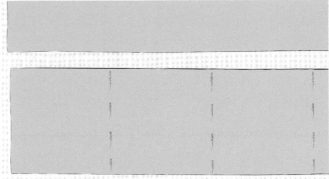

1 Make the 8½in (22cm) square template then cut 24 squares from each of your four contrasting fabrics. This gives you 96 squares in total, which will make 48 quilted squares – the finished throw is eight squares long and six squares wide.

2 Make your 7in (18cm) square template, then use it to cut out 48 squares of batting.

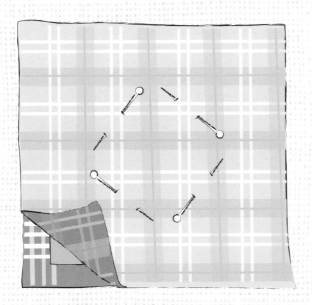

Tip You don't need to stick to the size shown here – make your throw bigger or smaller depending on what it's to be used for. You can even miss out the batting for a lightweight quilt or make it out of denim for a funky alternative.

3 Following the instructions for Rag quilting on pages 40–3, assemble your squares into quilt sandwiches, being sure to consistently pair the same two contrasting fabrics together.

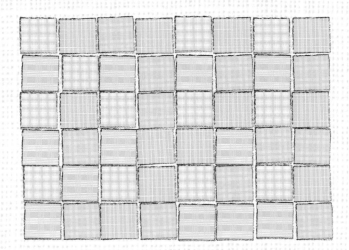

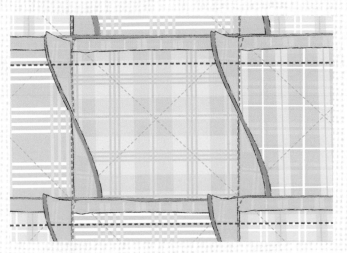

4 After you have completed step 3 on page 41 of the Rag quilting instructions, you will have 48 mini-quilt sandwiches. Spend some time arranging these into a rectangle that is eight squares long by six wide. When you are happy with the resulting pattern, continue with step 4 on page 41.

5 When sewing your strips together, push the top seams to the left and the bottom seams to the right so that each seam is twisted, as shown. This way, the strips all neatly slot together when they are sewn together (see Rag quilting, step 6, page 42).

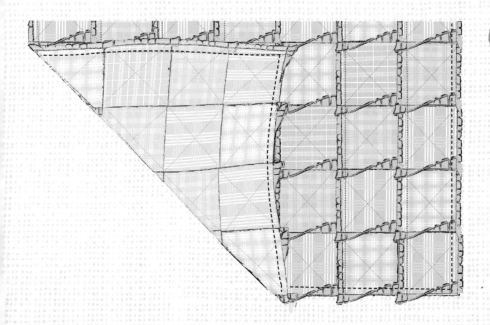

6 Run a final seam all the way around the edge of your throw. Use the same ¾in (2cm) you have used throughout and if you know your quilt will be getting some rough handling, then go around the edge twice.

HAND-TIED QUILTING

THIS FORM OF QUILTING GIVES A WONDERFULLY LIGHTWEIGHT FEEL AND HAPPENS TO BE ONE OF THE FASTEST METHODS OF SECURING QUILTED LAYERS. IT ALSO GIVES YOU THE OPPORTUNITY TO CUSTOMIZE YOUR QUILT TOP WITH UNIQUE YET FUNCTIONAL EMBELLISHMENTS.

Quilters use this technique to hold together batting and fabric instead of the more labour-intensive process of quilting with stitches. This technique can also be used when the layers to be secured are too thick to stitch through. Hand-tied quilts are less stiff, thicker and yet lighter than stitched quilts because the batting is not compressed by the stitching. They can also be warmer than stitched quilts, even when using the same amount of batting, as the air trapped inside acts as additional insulation.

To hand tie a quilt, use strong cotton thread and a large-eyed embroidery needle that is sharp and big enough to make a hole through the fabric and batting but will also pull through the thread without pulling the batting out with it. The knots used to secure the thread can be a feature in themselves or buttons or cutout shapes can be used to strengthen each knot and add decoration.

Hand tying a patchwork quilt is particularly effective because the repeating patchwork can either be tied in the patch's centre or in each corner where the blocks meet. This emphasizes the patches and ensures the quilt is tied at regular intervals.

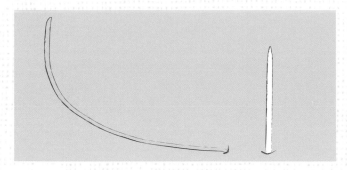

1 With a long strand of No.10 or 12 crochet cotton or embroidery perle thread, plunge your needle down through all the quilt layers. Leave a tail of about 3in (8cm) on the top surface. Bring the needle back up, about ¼in (6mm) from your tail. Keep your needle straight so it comes up in the right place.

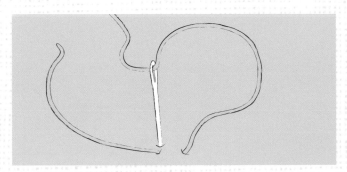

2 Plunge the needle back down through the sandwich, next to your tail of thread.

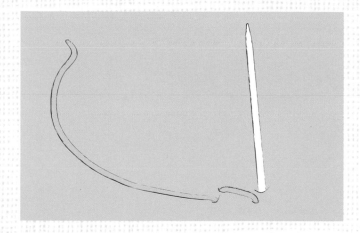

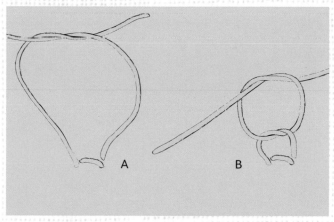

3   Come back up through the fabric, near to where you came up before.

4   Tie a reef knot by knotting the left over right (A) then right over left (B), as shown. Pull the knot tight, leaving a tail that is about 1in (2.5cm) long on each knot.

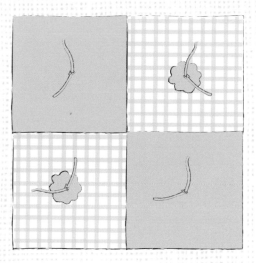

5   For added interest, you may want to add fabric shapes or buttons before you tie the reef knot. Choose a fabric that will not fray, such as felt, and pin it in place before you plunge through your sandwich.

6   Knots should be placed in rows about 6in (15cm) apart or less on a small project.

Project three

TEA COSY

THIS SIMPLE BUT STYLISH TEA COSY WILL PROVIDE YOU WITH PLENTY OF PRACTICE AT SEWING A CURVED SEAM AND HAND-TIED QUILTING. THE POLYESTER WADDING KEEPS THIS PRETTY TEA COSY LIGHTWEIGHT YET IT'S DELIGHTFULLY THICK AND SOFT – PERFECT FOR HIGH TEA!

YOU WILL NEED

- 30 x 24in (76 x 61cm) plain linen or cotton fabric
- Two 5in (13cm) squares of contrasting non-fray fabric such as wool or felt
- 26 x 20in (68 x 50cm) polyester wadding
- Matching general-purpose thread
- Perle embroidery thread in two complementary colours
- Contrasting buttons
- Dressmaking, paper and small needlework scissors
- Machine universal needle (size 90/14)
- Large-eye embroidery needle
- Quilting or dressmaking pins
- Thimble
- Seam ripper
- Craft knife, steel ruler and cutting mat
- Pencil, paper and marker pen
- Tea cosy and flower templates on page 115

FINISHED SIZE

13 x 10in (34 x 25cm)

TECHNIQUES USED

Tacking stitch (see page 20)
Pin for machine stitch (see page 19)
Seam allowance (see page 18)
Starting/finishing a stitch (see page 20)
Whip stitch (see page 21)
Hand-tied quilting (see page 48)

MATERIALS TO USE

Whether you want to use cotton or linen fabric here is a personal choice – it simply depends on what you think will look the nicest (and perhaps what kind of china you have...).

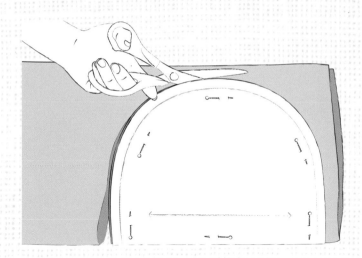

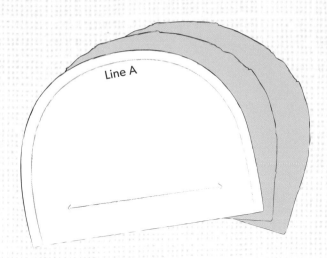

1 Fold your fabric in half along its width, so you have a long, thin rectangle. Make sure your fold is straight along the grain of the fabric. Pin your tea cosy pattern with the straight edge on the fold of the fabric and cut around. Cut two.

2 Trim your pattern to Line A. Pin it onto the wadding and cut; you do not need to place it on a fold, as you only want semicircles of wadding. Cut two.

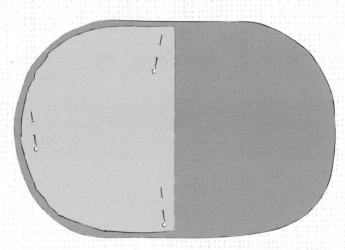

3 Open out your fabric pieces. You will have two elongated ovals. Place both ovals, RSD, onto a flat surface and pin one wadding semicircle onto each. Make sure the wadding is pinned ½in (12mm) from the edge of the fabric.

4 Tack the wadding semicircles onto the fabric ovals by stitching around the edge and diagonally across the wadding.

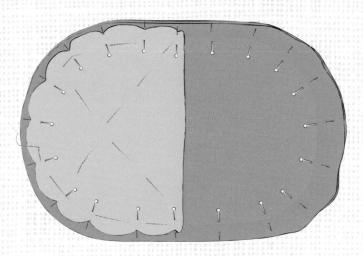

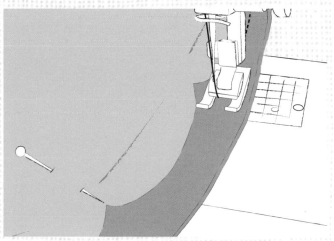

5 Lay one of your ovals, RSU, onto a flat surface and lay the second oval on top of it, RSD, so the right sides are facing each other (RST) and the halves with wadding are matched up. Make sure all the edges line up around the edge of the oval and pin for machine stitch.

6 Now it is time to sew most of the seam (note that you do not completely sew around the oval but leave a gap at the bottom). See step 7 overleaf for details before continuing. Choose a medium-length stitch and start at the half of the oval without wadding. Sew ½in (12mm) from the edge of the fabric. Once you get to the wadding, try not to stitch it into the seam; nudge it out of the way if necessary. Remember to take out each pin as you sew.

Tip Sewing around a curve is not especially difficult. Remember to watch the distance between the presser foot and the edge of the fabric and not the needle going up and down. Go slow and guide the material with your left hand, keeping the seam allowance consistent as you go.

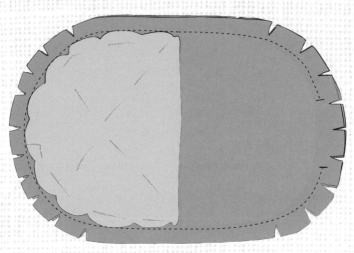

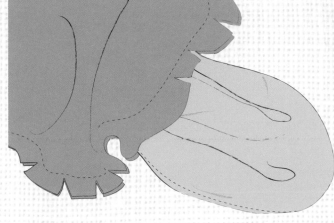

7 Do not sew all the way around the edge but leave a 4in (10cm) gap, as shown. Next, being careful not to snip your stitches, cut small V-shaped notches around the curved edges. These notches will stop the curved seam from puckering later.

8 Turn your tea cosy the right way out by gently pulling the inside out through the gap you have left in the seam. Do this a little bit at a time so you don't strain the stitches. Smooth out your oval and run your hand around the inside, pushing out the seams so the oval is as big as it can be.

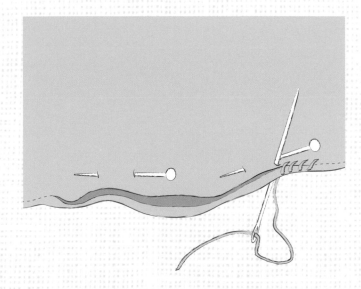

9 Your project will soon resemble a tea cosy. The side with no wadding is the lining and will be pushed up inside the wadded side. But first, you must sew up the gap. Tuck the raw edges inside and pin, then whip stitch the gap closed.

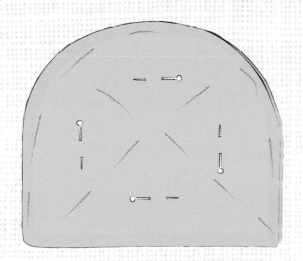

10 Push the lining up inside the two layers of wadding. Spend some time making sure it is not twisted and then pin in place. Do not take out the tacking stitches just yet.

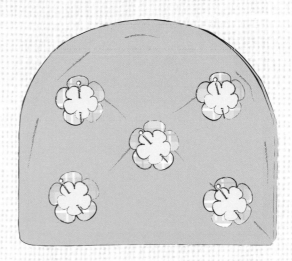

11 Take your flower paper patterns, pin them onto the non-fray fabric and cut out five large flowers and five small flowers. Pin them onto your tea cosy, as shown.

12 Following the hand-tied quilting instructions, use two strands of contrasting thread and add the flowers and button to decorate each knot. Tie each knot and added embellishments, as shown. Finally, take out your tacking.

Tip When adding embellishments to hand-tied quilting, string them onto the thread before you start each knot (tying a knot in the end of the thread will stop it falling off) and come up through the embellishment, flower shape and/or button when making your stitch.

STRIP PATCHWORK

THIS IS A POPULAR METHOD OF BUILDING A QUICK AND EASY QUILT TOP. IT IS ALSO A GREAT WAY TO USE UP ALL THOSE LEFTOVER SCRAPS OF FABRIC THAT ARISE FROM OTHER PROJECTS, ALLOWING YOU TO REALLY USE YOUR IMAGINATION WITH COLOUR AND PATTERN.

For this technique, you can use precisely cut strips of the same width or use random strips that just happen to be in your scrap bag. The resulting effect will be very different but, however you choose to cut the strips, the basic technique, which is sewing multiple strips of different fabrics together to form a patchwork quilt top, will remain the same.

Strip patchwork is a lovely technique for quilters of all skill levels, but is particularly good if you are new to patchwork quilting. It is quick and there are no seams to match up. The simple construction doesn't take too much concentration, which means you're able to really focus on choosing fabrics and experimenting with colours.

If you're nervous about putting colours together then it is possible to buy packs of pre-cut strips called Jelly Rolls (see page 14). The strips are usually 2½in (6.5cm) wide and the packs contain lots of different fabrics in complementary prints and colours. If you use a Jelly Roll for Strip patchwork, you are guaranteed a beautiful result.

Tip If this is the first time you have attempted Strip patchwork then go for random-sized strips rather than regular, as it is easier than trying to get all of the strips exactly the same size.

1 First cut your strips across the width of the fabric – or go to the shop and choose your Jelly Roll. The width of each strip depends on the project, but should be wider than 3in (8cm) if this is your first attempt.

2 Lay your strips RSU, on a flat surface, in the order in which you want to sew them together.

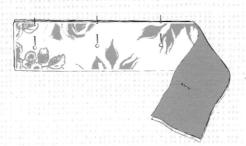
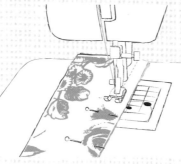
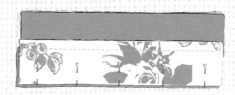

3 Take your first two strips and place one on top of the other, RST. Pin for machine stitch (see page 19).

4 Following the seam guide on your machine (see page 23), sew the strips together, leaving a ½in (12mm) seam allowance. After sewing, unpin, open up and lay back down in order. Repeat with the next pair of strips, and until all the strips are sewn into pairs.

5 Using the same method as in steps 3 and 4, pin and sew the pairs of strips together to make blocks of four. Holding them up in the air and letting them hang down before you pin, helps to keep them straight.

Tip It is very tempting to start at one end of the rows of strips and sew them together one by one until you get to the end. If done this way, it is very hard to stop the quilt from going wonky. It is much better to sew in pairs and then blocks as described. This helps to keep everything nice and straight.

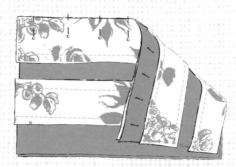

6 You will now have a number of blocks of four strips – exactly how many will depend on the size of your project. Pin and sew these blocks of four together – as in steps 3 and 4 – to form your quilt top.

7 Iron the seams flat (see page 19), making them all face the same way.

Project four

DUFFEL BAG

USE STRIP QUILTING TO MAKE THIS FUNKY DRAWSTRING DUFFEL BAG. ITS SIMPLE SQUARE BASE IS EASY TO MAKE AND, BEING QUILTED, IT CAN BE USED AS A COOL BAG. ROBUST JUTE WEBBING ALLOWS THE HANDLE TO TAKE THE STRAIN, EVEN IF THE BAG IS FILLED TO THE TOP.

YOU WILL NEED

- About 25 strips, each 21in (53cm) x 3½–6in (9–15cm), from a variety of fabrics
- 25 x 51in (64 x 130cm) and 13 x 13in (33 x 33cm) cotton lining fabric
- 22 x 52in (55 x 132cm) and 14 x 14in (36 x 36cm) cotton batting
- 95in (240cm) jute upholstery webbing
- Matching general-purpose thread
- Dressmaking, paper and small needlework scissors
- Machine universal needle (size 90/14)
- Machine quilting needle (size 90/14)
- Quilting or dressmaking pins
- Paper clip or safety pin
- Seam ripper
- Tape measure
- Craft knife, steel ruler and cutting mat
- Pencil, paper and marker pen
- 12in (30cm) square paper template

FINISHED SIZE

20in (50cm) height x 12in (30cm) depth x 12in (30cm) width

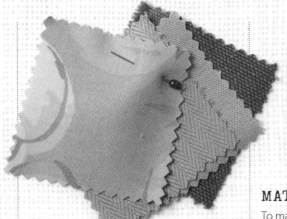

TECHNIQUES USED

Strip patchwork (see page 56)
Preparing the quilt sandwich (see page 26)
Parallel lines (see page 27)
Squaring up (see page 25)
Pin for machine stitch (see page 19)
Turning a corner (see page 23)
Binding edges (see page 28)

MATERIALS TO USE

To make a nice, strong bag, use slightly thicker fabrics than you would for a bed cover. Quantities of fabric depend on how many different prints or colours you choose to use, but the strips should be enough to construct two panels – one rectangle, measuring 21in x 51in (53 x 130cm) and one square, measuring 21 x 21in (53 x 53cm). Jute upholstery webbing makes a stronger handle and drawstring than making them from fabric.

Tip Your lining fabric will form the top border on the bag so make sure it is a fabric that complements your overall colour scheme.

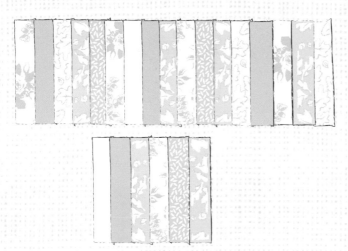

1 Using the strips you have cut and following the instructions for the Strip patchwork technique, construct your rectangular and square panels. Spend time arranging the strips before sewing them together.

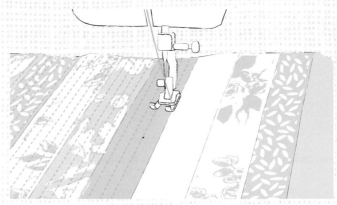

2 Prepare your quilt sandwiches, then quilt the top and batting together using the Parallel Lines technique.

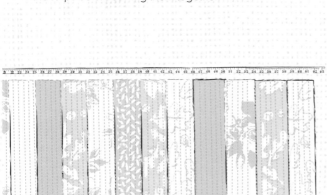

3 Now square up the rectangular panel. It needs to be 19 x 51in (48 x 129cm).

4 Cut a 12in (30cm) square paper template, then pin this onto your oversized square quilted panel RSD on a flat surface and draw around your template. Leaving 1in (2.5cm) extra for the seam allowance, cut around your template. This will be the base of the bag.

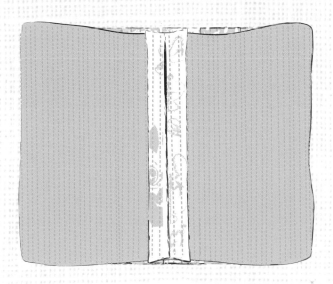

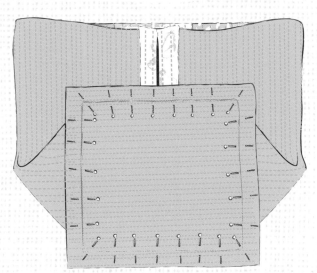

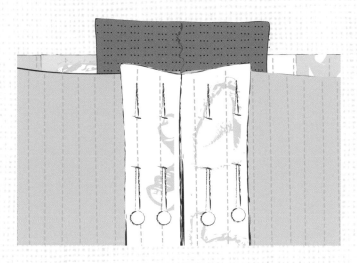

5 Fold your rectanglular panel in half lengthways, RST, and pin for machine stitch. Using the guide on your machine, leave a 1in (2.5cm) seam allowance and sew together. Press the seam open. You have made the tube that forms the body of the bag.

Tip Remember to iron all your seams flat (see page 19), facing the same way. This will make it much easier to sew the bag together when you get to that stage.

6 Join the tube you have created to the square base, making sure you have RST and that you have lined up the edges of the fabric. Pin the seam of the tube to the centre of one of the sides of the square first, then continue pinning all the way around. Ease the corners into place.

7 For the handle, cut about 24in (60cm) of jute upholstery webbing. Slide this up inside of your fabric tube, sliding the end through, between the square base and the tube just at the bottom of the side seam. Make sure it sticks out above the tube by about 1in (2.5cm) as shown. Pin securely.

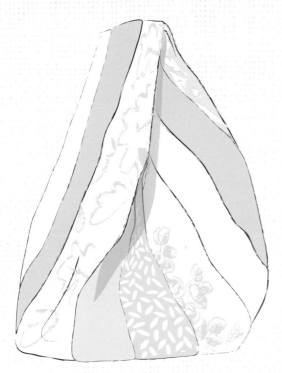

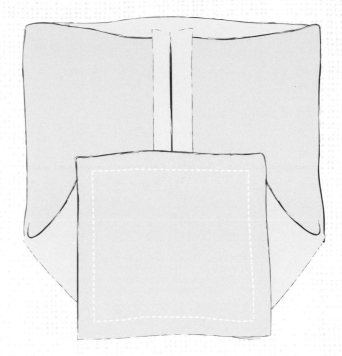

8 Leaving a 1in (2.5cm) seam allowance, machine stitch around the square base to attach it to the tube, following the line you have drawn – this will involve turning corners. Turn the bag the right way out.

9 Next you need to make the lining of the bag. Using the two panels of lining fabric you have cut, follow steps 4 to 8 to construct a lining tube and base minus a handle. You will notice the lining is taller than the quilted bag.

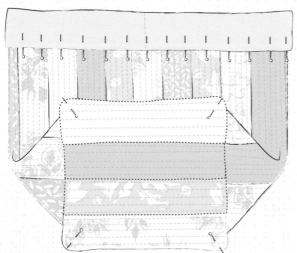

10 Leaving the lining with the seams facing outwards, slide it inside the quilted bag. Keep the side seams of the lining and outer bag lined up. Pin the bottom corners of the lining to the bottom corners of the outer bag. Fold the edge of the lining over the edge of the outer bag, then fold the raw edges of the lining under by at least 1in (2.5cm). The overlapping border needs to be at least 3in (8cm). Pin for machine stitch.

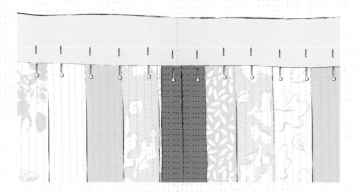

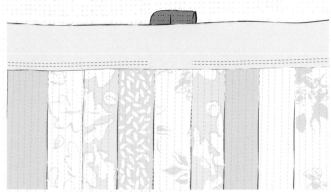

11 Remove a couple of pins from the border and slip the other end of the webbing under it, making sure it isn't twisted, then pin in place.

12 Starting opposite the handle, run a double row of machine stitching around the bag to secure the lining and the handle at the same time, being sure to leave a 3in (8cm) gap between the beginning and end of the stitching.

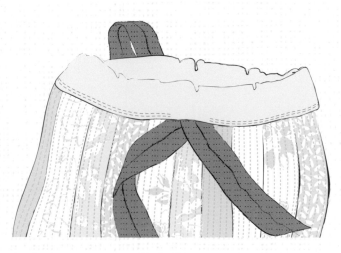

13 Using the gap you have left, thread the drawstring through this hem, tying the webbing to a large paper clip or safety pin to help guide it through. Finally, trim the ends of the webbing and stitch across each end to stop them fraying.

Tip To make sure your handle can take the strain of a heavy load, double up the stitching when you stitch over the jute webbing as you are attaching the square base and lining. Do this by reverse stitching (see page 22) a couple of times on top of the webbing.

SIMPLE QUILT BLOCK

THE BASIC COMPONENT OF PATCHWORK QUILTING IS THE QUILT BLOCK. ONCE YOU HAVE MASTERED THE ABILITY TO CONSTRUCT A QUILT BLOCK ACCURATELY, TACKLING A FULL-SIZED PATCHWORK QUILT WILL BE WITHIN REACH.

When you look at a completed patchwork quilt with its striking combinations of complex geometric shapes, it may seem nearly impossible to tell how it was constructed. But the secret to how these intricate designs are put together lies in building up patterns of quilt blocks.

A quilt block is simply a small section of the whole top; it is usually square and made up of small pieces of fabric sewn together. Multiple, identical blocks are made and then sewn together to form the geometric patterns. There are thousands upon thousands of different types of blocks, some traditional, some contemporary, and more are invented every day. It is this infinite variety that attracts many people to patchwork quilting.

The Nine Patch quilt block is one of the simplest, and constructing this block will give you plenty of practice in machine sewing. For ease, I have increased the traditional quilter's seam allowance from ¼in (6mm) to ½in (12mm). By starting with just nine simple squares you will also get the practice you need in sewing consistent seams. Once you have mastered the ability to sew accurately, you can reduce your seam allowance to the traditional quilter's ¼in (6mm), which makes the finished quilt less bulky and reduces wastage.

I have also included the Disappearing Nine Patch block within this technique, as it is a development of the Nine Patch and a great demonstration of a block that looks really complicated but that is actually very simple. To demonstrate this technique I have used a 5½in (14cm) square that reduces down to 4½in (11.5cm) after sewing the ½in (12mm) seams.

Tip Keeping to a consistent seam allowance is the key to successful patchwork, as all the squares need to be the same size so they line up when sewn together.

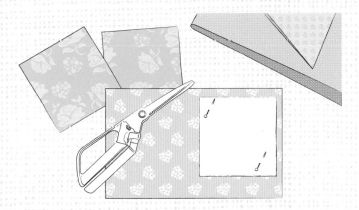

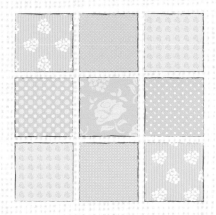

1 Carefully cut a 5½in (14cm) square paper template. If you are going to cut the squares from nine different fabrics, pin your template to the fabric and cut around. If you are cutting multiple squares from the same fabric, see Project Two's tip on page 44 for how to quickly cut rows of squares.

2 Arrange your squares; this is a personal choice, but if you are making a Disappearing Nine Patch block (see step 10, page 67), it is good to have a strong-coloured patch in the centre. For more on choosing fabric, see pages 14–15.

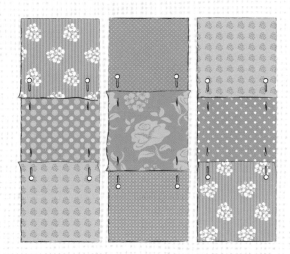

3 Working in columns of three, RST, pin three squares together for machine stitch (see page 19). Sew to form strips. Remember to use a ½in (12mm) seam allowance and reverse stitch when you start and finish stitching to secure.

4 With RSD, press the seams flat. Iron the central strip with both seams pointing towards the outside edges. Iron the outer strips with the seams facing the centre of the strip.

5 Next you need to sew these three strips together to form your quilt block. Leave the three strips RSD, in the order you wish to sew them. Take one outer strip and the central strip and put one on top of the other with RST. Line up the seams, which should be facing in opposite directions, and pin for machine stitch. Machine stitch this seam, leaving an ½in (12mm) seam allowance. Then repeat with the last strip. Keep double checking that you have pinned the side together that you wish to sew.

6 Once you have ironed the seams, pointing inwards, you can turn your square RSU to view your simple Nine Patch quilt block. You can now make as many blocks as are needed then square up each one (see page 25) before sewing them together.

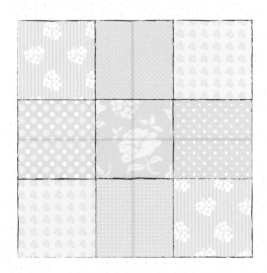

7 To go on to make a Disappearing Nine Patch, first accurately fold your Nine Patch quilt block in half, ironing the crease along the fold. Open the block and fold the other way; again, iron along the fold. Carefully cut your block in half and then in half again using the ironed creases as a guide.

Tip When matching seams to sew together, if the two seams are ironed flat in opposite directions they naturally slot together and it is easier to make sure your seams match up.

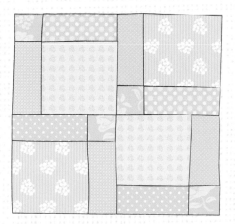
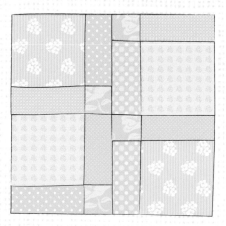
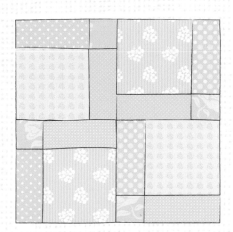

8 These four squares can now be rearranged to create a variety of different patterns.

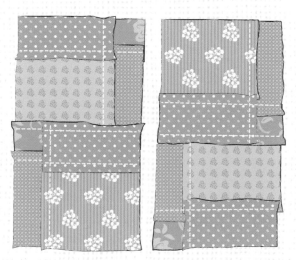

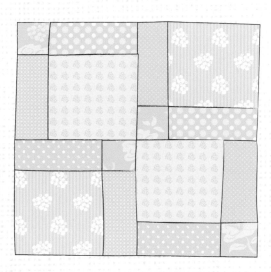

9 Working in columns, pin and machine stitch two of your squares together. There will be no seams to match, but make sure the existing seams stay flat as you sew over them. Iron the new seam flat, pointing upwards. Repeat the step with the other two squares. This time when you iron the seam, make it point downwards (see page 19).

10 Sew your two columns together again to form a square, matching the central seam. The seams, if ironed correctly, should be pointing in opposite directions, creating a nice, neat, straight central join. Iron your last seam open and square up ready for use in your project.

Project five

TABLE MAT

THIS IS A QUICK AND SIMPLE PROJECT THAT LETS YOU CONCENTRATE ON BASIC TECHNIQUES WHILE CREATING A USEFUL AND PRETTY TABLE MAT. IT IS ESPECIALLY NICE TO BE ABLE TO PRACTISE HAND STITCHING THE BINDING BEFORE EMBARKING ON MORE AMBITIOUS PROJECTS.

YOU WILL NEED

- Nine 5½in (14cm) squares of fabric
- 15 x 15in (38 x 38cm) backing fabric
- 65in (162cm) of 2½in- (6cm) wide strips of same fabric used for backing fabric
- 15 x 15in (38 x 38cm) cotton batting
- Matching general-purpose thread
- Contrasting quilting thread
- Dressmaking, paper and small needlework scissors
- Machine universal needle (size 90/14)
- No.9 hand-stitch quilting needle
- No.9 sharp or embroidery needle
- Quilting or dressmaking pins
- Thimble
- Seam ripper
- Tape measure
- Craft knife, steel ruler and cutting mat
- Pencil and paper
- 5½in (14cm) square paper template

FINISHED SIZE

14 x 14in (36 x 36cm)

TECHNIQUES USED

Simple quilt block (see page 64)
Squaring up (see page 25)
Preparing the quilt sandwich (see page 26)
Running, quilting and tacking stitch (see page 20)
Outline quilting (see page 27)
Binding edges (see page 28)

MATERIALS TO USE

Any project that is designed for use in the kitchen needs to be made of a robust, washable fabric. It is also best to use cotton batting as this will protect your surfaces against heat better than polyester.

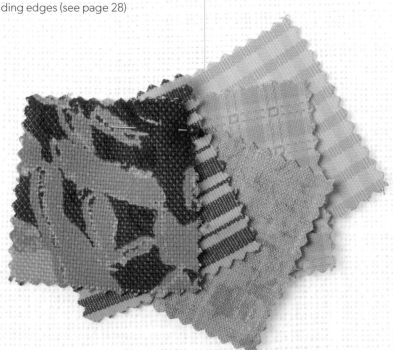

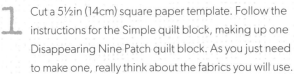

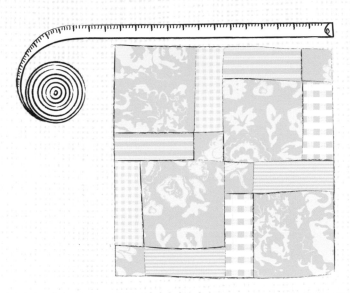

1 Cut a 5½in (14cm) square paper template. Follow the instructions for the Simple quilt block, making up one Disappearing Nine Patch quilt block. As you just need to make one, really think about the fabrics you will use.

2 Square up your quilt block. If you find this difficult, cut out a paper template and cut around it.

3 Prepare your quilt sandwich. This can be held together with pins rather than tacking or safety pins, as it is only small. Remember to leave the backing fabric and batting bigger than the quilt block.

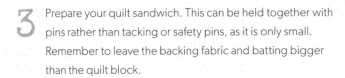

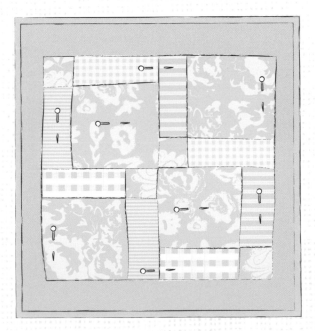

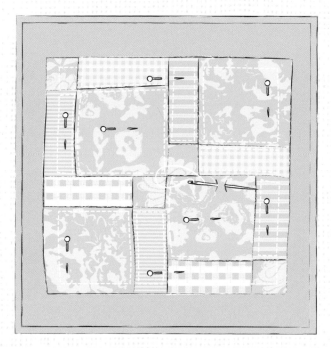

4 Use running or quilting stitch to Outline quilt each of the patches to secure the three layers together. You need to stitch about ¼in (6mm) from the seams to emphasize the shape of the patches nicely, but remember you still have to attach the binding, so your stitching should be ¾in (2cm) from the outer edges to leave room for the binding seam allowance.

5 Trim your backing fabric and batting so they are level with the quilt block and then, using the straight strips of backing fabric, follow the instructions for binding your work to complete your table mat.

Tip A set of these single blocks make great place mats or sew two together to make a basic oven glove!

SPEED PIECING

THIS TECHNIQUE IS THE QUILTER'S SECRET TO MAKING MULTIPLE PIECES FOR PATCHWORKING QUICKLY AND ACCURATELY. THERE ARE MANY DIFFERENT WAYS OF SPEED PIECING AND HERE I SHOW YOU HOW TO MAKE TRIANGLE SQUARES.

Expert quilters are a crafty lot and are always looking for ways to speed things up. Some of the more intricate quilts are made up of many hundreds of tiny squares, triangles or other shapes, so who wouldn't want to find a way to make the cutting and sewing more accurate and a little bit quicker? The simplest type of Speed Piecing is when you sew two narrow strips together to form a long wider strip, which is then cut into squares consisting of two rectangles.

If you get bitten by the quilting bug, it would be a good idea to invest in a rotary cutter and quilter's ruler to use when you are Speed Piecing. These tools enable you to cut and piece together large projects quicker and more accurately than it seems possible to a beginner. I have, however, stuck to the scissors and paper template method here, as it is good to be able to learn the basics without the cost of extra gadgets and without worrying about how to use them effectively.

This technique introduces you to Speed Piecing squares made from two half-square triangles (a triangle made from cutting a square in half); these are also known as triangle squares or HSTs. It's a useful trick to know, as triangles can be tricky to cut accurately. The technique enables you to make two triangle squares from two larger contrasting fabric squares. Triangle squares can then be assembled in a variety of different ways to form different patterns.

I have used a ¼in (6mm) seam allowance for this technique rather than the larger ½in (12mm) seam allowance I've been using, as the way these squares are sewn makes it achievable for all skill levels.

ROTARY CUTTER

You might want to invest in a rotary cutter (a small gadget with a sharp circular blade) to use with a cutting mat and a steel ruler. It is useful for cutting through several layers of fabric and for cutting long, straight strips when making binding (see page 28).

1 The size of your squares will depend on your project, but here I have used a 6in (15cm) square. First cut an accurate 6in (15cm) paper template, which can be used as a guide to cut two 6in (15cm) squares from contrasting fabrics.

2 Place the lightest-coloured fabric RSD on a flat surface. Using a ruler, draw a pencil line diagonally from corner to corner across the fabric. Make sure you draw your line on the wrong side of the fabric!

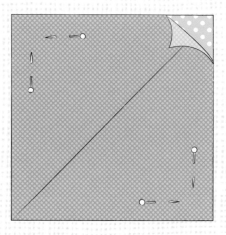

3 Place the two squares of fabric RST, with the lighter fabric on the top, on a flat surface. Make sure all the corners are lined up and pin together. Avoid pinning across the pencil line.

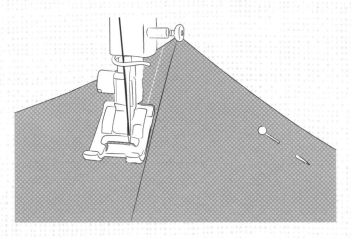
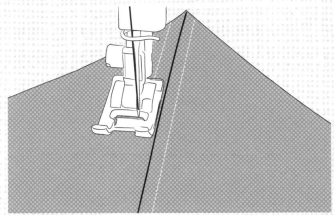

4 Place your square on the sewing machine with the right side of the foot just resting on the guideline – you shall be sewing diagonally across the square using the pencil line as your guide. Slowly start to stitch, making sure the foot stays parallel to the line. Assuming that you are using a standard-sized foot, your seam will automatically be ¼in (6mm) away from the pencil guideline.

5 Stitch along the opposite side of the pencil line, again keeping the stitching ¼in (6mm) away from the pencil line. You will now have two rows of stitches ½in (12mm) apart.

Tip Don't worry if your sewing machine foot is not exactly ¼in (6mm) wide. The important thing is consistency. As long as you use the same measurement throughout the whole technique and project it doesn't matter if it is a little less than ¼in (6mm) or a little more.

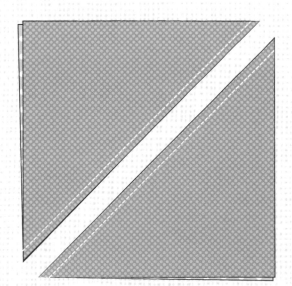

6 Cut along the pencil line to end up with two triangles.

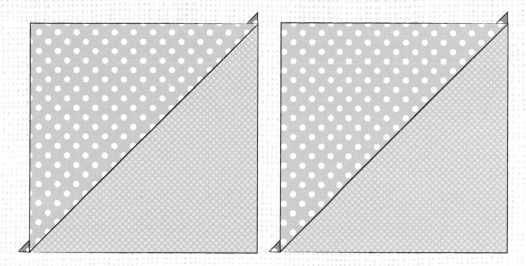

7   Open out the two triangle squares. Iron flat, with the seam facing towards the darker fabric. Make as many triangle squares as you need for your project.

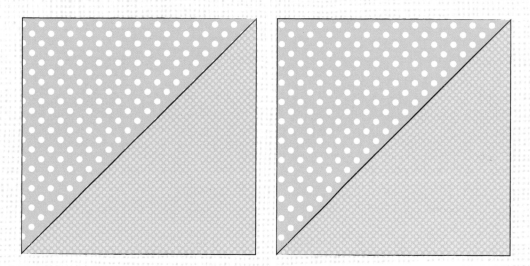

8   Snip off the dog ears (those little triangles of seam allowance) that are poking out and showing from the right side of the square. You have your finished triangle squares.

PINBOARD

MAKING THIS EYE-CATCHING PATCHWORK PINBOARD WILL CERTAINLY SHOWCASE YOUR
NEWLY ACQUIRED QUILTING SKILLS AND IT'S A FANTASTIC WAY TO DECORATE BEAUTIFULLY
WHAT IS OFTEN SIMPLY THOUGHT OF AS A FUNCTIONAL ITEM.

YOU WILL NEED

- 18 squares, 4⅞in (12cm) each, of a light, plain cotton fabric
- 18 squares, 4⅞in (12cm) each, of a dark printed cotton fabric
- 16 x 16in (40 x 40cm) polyester wadding
- Matching general-purpose thread
- Thick yarn or string
- Five self-covered buttons, covered in your chosen fabric
- 16 x 16in (40 x 40cm) picture frame
- 16 x 16in (40 x 40cm) corkboard ¼in (6mm) thick
- Dressmaking, paper and small needlework scissors
- Machine universal needle (size 90/14)
- Quilting or dressmaking pins
- Thimble
- Tape measure
- Craft knife, steel ruler and cutting mat
- Pencil
- Paper

FINISHED SIZE

16 x 16in (40 x 40cm)

TECHNIQUES USED

Speed piecing (see page 72)
Simple quilt block (see page 64)
Hand-tied quilting (see page 48)

MATERIALS TO USE

This project is most effective if you keep to using just two different fabrics, creating the star pattern shown. I've also chosen to use polyester wadding here to give the board a much puffier look but you could use cotton batting if you wish.

1 Cut a 4⅞ x 4⅞ in (12 x 12cm) square paper template. Use it to cut out 18 light-coloured squares and 18 dark-coloured squares from your fabric.

2 Following the instructions for Speed Piecing, make up your 36 triangle squares.

Tip To quickly and accurately cut your squares of fabric, cut strips across the width of your fabric. Then, using your template as a guide, cut these strips into squares. To speed things up you can cut two layers of fabric at once.

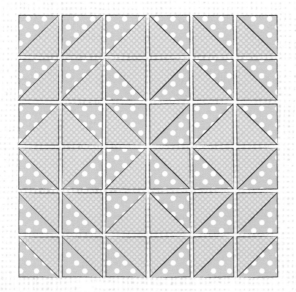

3 Arrange your squares in a 6 x 6 grid. To replicate the pattern of the illustrated pinboard, lay out your squares as shown.

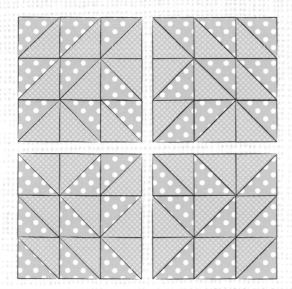

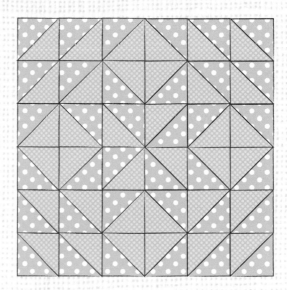

4 For the next stage, think of your squares as four separate Nine Patch quilt blocks. Follow the instructions for the Simple quilt block, to assemble your quilt blocks together, but use a ¼in (6mm) seam allowance instead of ½in (12mm).

5 Sew your four quilt blocks together, using the same method as described in step 9 of the Simple quilt block technique. Don't forget to iron all the seams.

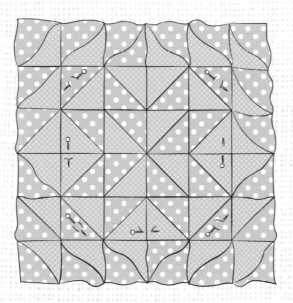

6 Place your polyester wadding onto a flat surface. Mark the centre of the square. Place your quilt top, centrally, on top of the wadding and pin to secure.

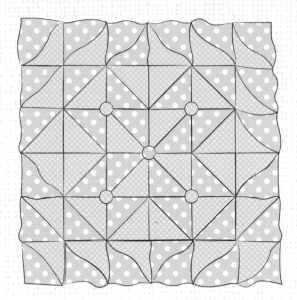

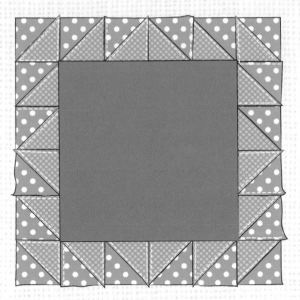

7 Use the Hand-tied quilting technique to secure the quilt top to the wadding, using the fabric-covered buttons as embellishments. Position as shown.

8 Turn over the quilt top and the attached wadding and place the corkboard on top. Make sure the corkboard is facing towards the wadding.

Tip Self-covered buttons are simple to use. Cut a circle of fabric, approximately ½in (12mm) bigger than the button you wish to cover. Place the button in the centre of the fabric, then fold the fabric over and hook it into the serrated edge. Work all the way around the button, hooking material over the serrated edge before snapping the back into place.

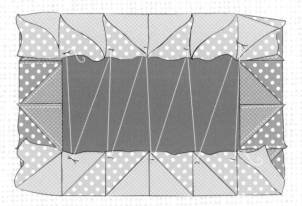

9 Fold over the top and bottom edges, then, using a long piece of yarn and a large-eyed needle, zig-zag from top to bottom to attach the quilt top and wadding to the corkboard. Try to go through the seams if possible, where there is a double thickness of fabric. Pull tight and secure.

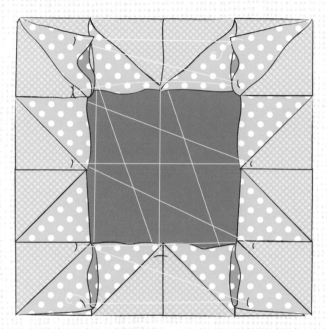

10 Turn your pinboard over and check there are no wrinkles, then repeat step 9 to secure the sides.

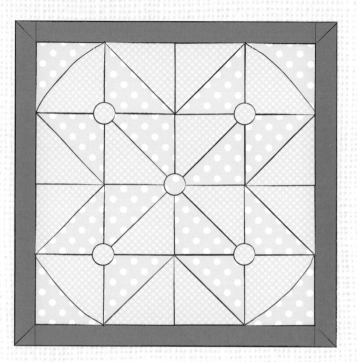

11 Place the completed panel into your picture frame and hang in a prominent position for all to admire.

Tip If you don't have a picture frame exactly the right size, it is very easy to adapt this project to make a pinboard to fit the size of frame you do have, or make the pinboard and hang it without a frame.

LONDON STAIRS

THIS IS ONE OF MY ALL-TIME FAVOURITE PATCHWORK PATTERNS. IT BUILDS ON THE BASIC STRIP
PATCHWORK METHOD TO MAKE QUILT BLOCKS BASED ON TWO ALTERNATING RECTANGLES.
IT'S SIMPLE, EFFECTIVE AND ELEGANT AND SUITS A WIDE RANGE OF QUILTING PROJECTS.

Endless Stairs, Virginia Worm Fence, Winding Stairs and Attic Stairs are some of the names this traditional quilt block is known by, depending upon what part of the world you come from. As I come from the UK, I like to refer to this pattern as London Stairs.

The sheer variety of names it is known by is evidence of what a popular quilting pattern it has been for generations. What I find fascinating about traditional quilting techniques is that quilters have been stitching the very same pattern over and over again for many years and yet each and every quilt created is unique due to the fabric that the quilter has chosen.

Some people construct this block using one plain fabric, which creates the stairs, and then alternate this with a myriad of different-patterned fabrics. Others choose to form the stairs using a variety of dark fabrics and alternate these with various lighter prints. Yet another option is to use two plain, vibrant colours to create a contemporary, zig-zag effect. Quilters will

tell you that making the decision about what fabrics you want to use in your design can be more difficult than the actual sewing. In fact, be warned: many an hour can be spent in a fabric shop staring at rolls of fabric trying to decide which ones to buy...

Tip When you look at just one block on its own it is hard to see the staircase effect, but as soon as you sew the blocks together, the effect becomes apparent.

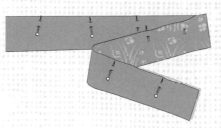
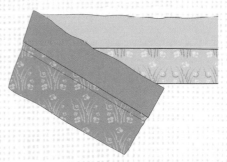

1 Take two strips of contrasting fabric, both of equal widths; how wide will depend on the project you are working on. For this demonstration I have used 3½in (9cm) strips.

2 Place the two contrasting strips, RST, onto a flat surface. Make sure the edges are lined up and pin for machine stitch (see page 19).

3 Using the guide on your sewing machine (see page 23), sew your strip together, being sure to leave a ½in (12mm) seam allowance. Iron your strips with the seams facing the darker fabric.

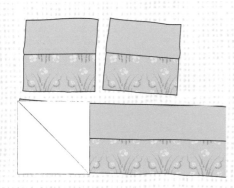

4 Cut out a 6in (15cm) square template and use this to cut your strip into 6in (15cm) squares. You have now constructed the basic square pieces needed for a London Stairs quilt top.

5 Your squares now need to be sewn together. Arrange them in blocks of four, as shown.

6 Refer back to the Simple quilt block technique (see page 64), for instructions on how to sew blocks together. For this block, note that you are only sewing four squares together, so press the seams in alternate directions.

PLAY MAT

THIS SQUARE PLAY MAT SHOWS THAT PATCHWORK QUILTS DON'T ALWAYS HAVE TO BE MADE
FROM LOTS OF DIFFERENT PRINTS AND COLOURS. IT IS SIMPLY MADE, USING TWO PLAIN LINENS
IN COMPLEMENTARY TONES, SHOWING THE LONDON STAIRS BLOCK TO GREAT EFFECT.

YOU WILL NEED

- 35 x 45in (90 x 114cm) cream linen
- 35 x 45in (90 x 114cm) taupe linen
- 41 x 41in (104 x 104cm) cream linen
  (backing fabric)
- Four 41 x 3in (104 x 8cm) strips
  backing fabric
- 41 x 41in (104 x 104cm) cotton batting
- Matching general-purpose thread
- Dressmaking, paper and small
  needlework scissors
- Machine universal needle (size 90/14)
- Machine quilting needle (size 90/14)
- No.9 sharp or embroidery needle
- Quilting or dressmaking pins
- Thimble
- Seam ripper
- Tape measure
- Craft knife, steel ruler and cutting mat
- Pencil and paper

FINISHED SIZE

36 x 36in (91 x 91cm)

TECHNIQUES USED

London Stairs quilt block (see page 82)

Simple quilt block (see page 64)

Preparing the quilt sandwich
(see page 26)

Tacking (see page 20)

Stitch in the Ditch (see page 27)

Binding edges (see page 28)

MATERIALS TO USE

This project uses a hardwearing linen
fabric that washes well. The staircase
pattern is subtly picked out in muted
creams, demonstrating that you only
need slightly different colours to create
pattern within a quilt.

Tip For a dramatically
different effect, use two bright,
zingy complementary colours
such as orange and lime green.

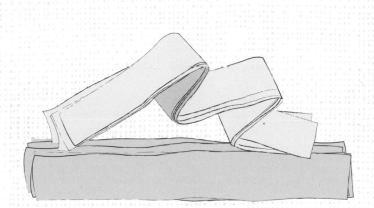

1 If using 45in (112cm) wide fabric, cut 10, 3¼in (8.5cm) strips from each of your contrasting fabrics. If your fabric is wider then you will need fewer strips. Cut across the width of the fabric. Cut a 5½in (14cm) square paper template.

2 Referring back to the London Stairs technique and using your template as a guide to cutting out the fabric, construct 64 basic squares. Always match the two contrasting fabrics together. Be sure to iron with the seams facing towards the darker fabric.

3 Keep following the London Stairs technique, steps 5 and 6, to construct 16 London Stairs blocks from the 64 basic blocks. When ironing the central seams, press eight flat to the left and eight flat to the right.

4 These 16 blocks now need to be sewn together. Referring to the illustration on the right, arrange four of your blocks with the stair pattern and seams lining up, as they need to be sewn together. Sew these four blocks together. Repeat with the remaining 12 blocks to form four larger blocks.

Tip Building up a patchwork quilt top from these simple squares made from strips makes it clear how the patterns on large quilt tops are constructed. Try making squares with three different fabric strips and even more patterns can be formed.

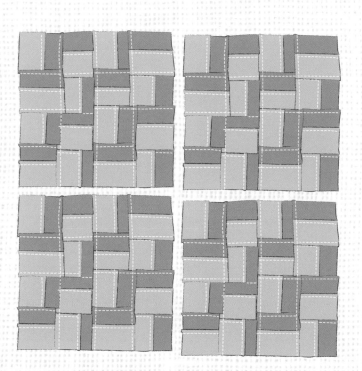

5 Now the squares are sewn into four larger blocks, the 'staircase' should be more obvious.

6 These four blocks need to be sewn together to form the quilt top, as in the Simple quilt block technique. Again, press the seams in alternate directions so they fit nicely together. Before going any further, square up your quilt top.

7 Now you can prepare your quilt sandwich. For this size of project, I recommend tacking the layers together.

8 Finally it is time to quilt the project. The basic Stitch in the Ditch method is best for this mat. Remove the tacking stitches when the quilting is complete.

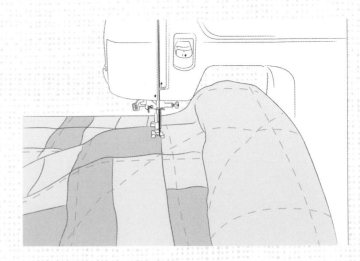

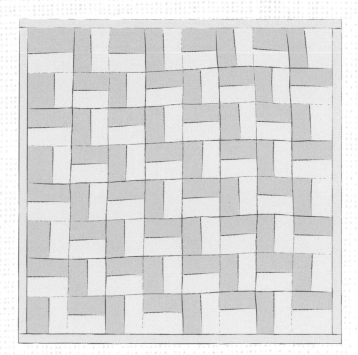

Tip If you have used a thick linen when binding the edges there will be quite a few layers to sew through. If your sewing machine struggles to get through them all, then hand stitch the corners, using hemming stitch (see page 21).

9 Trim the excess backing fabric and batting so all your layers are the same dimensions and then bind the edges of the mat. Instead of hand-stitching the hem, run a line of machine stitching close to the edge of the binding.

WHOLE CLOTH QUILTING

THIS BEAUTIFUL AND EFFECTIVE TECHNIQUE RELIES ON HAND-STITCHED QUILTING TO DRAW INTRICATE PATTERNS ACROSS THE SURFACE OF THE QUILT TOP, OFTEN WITH NO PATCHWORK, SO THE STITCHING CAN BE APPRECIATED WITHOUT DISTRACTION.

This quilting technique is now less popular than patchwork or other quilting done on the machine, mainly because it is extremely time consuming. But it has a beauty that relies totally on the design of the quilting.

Whole Cloth quilts were traditionally made in the north of England and Wales and created from one continuous piece of fabric. Like most historic crafts, this would have been a cheap, readily available fabric such as cotton. The exception to this rule was a 'stripy', which used wide strips of contrasting fabric, as they would have been cheaper to buy than the wide lengths of continuous fabric.

Tip This technique can be used to quilt a pre-printed fabric. Choose a fabric with a bold design, assemble it into a quilt sandwich and stitch around the printed pattern, using contrasting thread to emphasize the quilting – a really quick and easy way to add your own touch to a commercially designed fabric.

QUILTING HOOP

Some quilters, when tackling a large project, prefer to hand quilt using a quilting hoop to keep the three layers taut. But you won't need this for a small project, as long as the layers are securely tacked together.

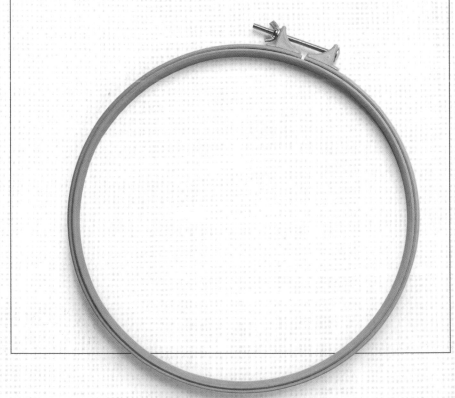

Whole Cloth quilts often had a central motif surrounded by an area of infill patterns, sometimes based around a specific design called the Running Durham Feather Stitch. The quilts could then have a decorated border worked around the edge.

For Whole Cloth quilting, the pattern is marked out onto the fabric before the quilt sandwich is assembled. It is possible to buy pre-printed Whole Cloth quilt tops or stencils that can be used to mark the pattern onto your chosen fabric. Alternatively, you can design your own pattern or find a printed template and transfer the pattern onto the fabric with the aid of some tracing paper.

Once marked up, the quilt top is assembled into a quilt sandwich in exactly the same way as other quilting techniques and the whole surface is hand stitched with quilting stitches, securing the three layers together and picking out the design.

It is well worth investing the time in this technique, as the results are absolutely beautiful. The tiny stitches give a subtlety that is hard to achieve on a machine and the technique has a quiet, meditative quality to it that is remarkably relaxing.

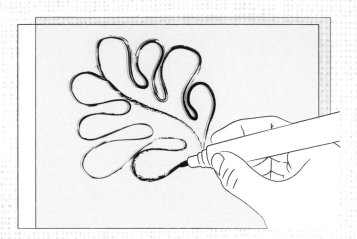

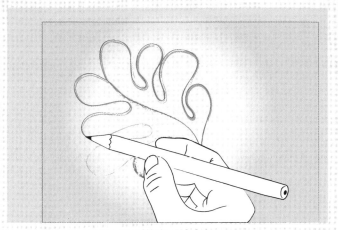

1 First you need to transfer your design onto your fabric. There are many ways of doing this and every quilter has their favourite. The following technique works well for a small project when using light-coloured fabric. Place a sheet of tracing paper over your motif and trace the design using a black permanent marker.

2 Tape your tracing paper onto a light box or window. Now tape your material over the top of the tracing paper, positioning it where you wish the motif to be. Carefully draw the motif onto the fabric with a soft sharp pencil or a light, washable felt-tip pen (always check it will wash out of the fabric you are using).

3 Take your fabric and assemble it into a quilt sandwich (see page 26). Secure with tacking stitches (see page 20).

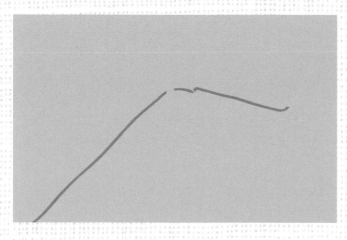

4 Using an embroidery needle and No.10 cotton crochet thread, refer to starting and finishing a stitch (see page 20) to secure your thread to the back of your quilt sandwich by taking a couple of stitches on top of one another.

5 Bring your needle to the front of your quilt sandwich and stitch even quilting stitches (see page 20) along the pencil lines to secure your three layers. Weave the needle in and out of the fabric to take more than one stitch at a time.

6 When the whole motif has been completely secured with quilting stitch, the tacking stitches can be removed and the project can be finished off and gently washed to remove the pencil lines.

CUSHION

THIS CUSHION COVER USES THE WHOLE CLOTH QUILTING TECHNIQUE TO PRODUCE
A BEAUTIFULLY TEXTURED SURFACE. USE A HARDWEARING COTTON WITH A WIDE STRIPE
FOR A LOOK REMINISCENT OF TRADITIONAL STRIPY QUILTS.

YOU WILL NEED

- Two squares 20 x 20in (50 x 50cm) and one rectangle 20 x 27in (50 x 70cm) cut from white, hardwearing cotton with a wide red stripe or from utility tea towels
- Red and white No. 8 cotton crochet thread
- 20 x 20in (50 x 50cm) calico
- 20 x 20in (50 x 50cm) cotton batting
- 20 x 20in (50 x 50cm) cushion pad
- Matching general-purpose thread
- Dressmaking, paper and small needlework scissors
- Machine universal needle (size 90/14)
- No.5 embroidery needle
- Quilting or dressmaking pins
- Thimble
- Seam ripper
- Tape measure
- Craft knife, steel ruler and cutting mat
- Pencil, tracing paper and black marker
- Flower template on page 114

FINISHED SIZE

20 x 20in (50 x 50cm)

TECHNIQUES USED

Whole Cloth quilting (see page 90)
Preparing the quilt sandwich (see page 26)
Running, tacking and quilting stitch (see page 20)
Pin for machine stitch (see page 19)
Starting and finishing a machine stitch (see page 22)
Turning a corner (see page 23)

MATERIALS TO USE

Traditional cotton or linen tea towels are the perfect size for this project and come with a stripe that will border the flower design. To prepare the fabric, use a seam ripper to undo the seams around the tea towel, and iron it flat. Calico, which is a cheap utility fabric, is used as the backing fabric as it will not be seen inside the cushion cover.

Tip If you need to adapt the size, cushion covers are usually made 1in (2.5cm) smaller than the internal pad, so measure your pad and then start with a square the same size. When you take into consideration the ½in (12mm) seam allowance needed, the finished cover will be 1in (2.5cm) smaller than the pad.

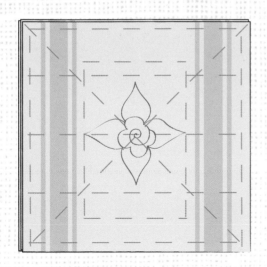

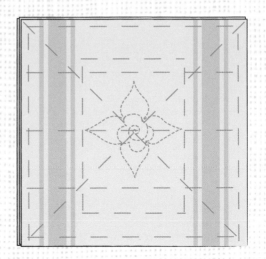

1 Take one 20 x 20in (50 x 50cm) square of the white cotton fabric. Referring back to step 1 of the Whole Cloth quilting technique, transfer the flower motif onto your fabric. Then assemble your fabric, batting and calico backing fabric into a quilt sandwich. Tack to secure, as shown.

2 Again, following the Whole Cloth quilting instructions, stitch around all of the pencil lines to complete the flower motif using the red No.8 cotton crochet thread.

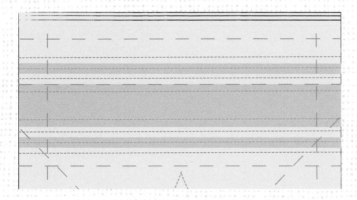

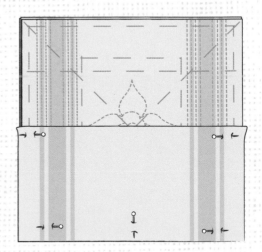

3 Run lines of running stitches along the stripes in a contrasting crochet thread. When all your quilting stitching is complete, remove the tacking stitches.

4 To assemble your cushion cover, place the completed quilted panel, RSU on a flat surface. Take your second 20 x 20in (50 x 50cm) square and fold it in half, WST, to form a rectangle. Place it on top of the panel, lining up any stripes and ensuring the fold is in the panel's centre.

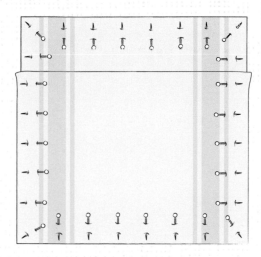

5 Fold the large rectangle and place it on top of these, again with the folded edge towards the square's centre. These two rectangles now overlap and form an 'envelope' which will hold the cushion pad. Pin for machine stitch around the square's edges, securing all layers and checking the stripes are lined up.

6 Using the guide on your sewing machine, sew right around the edge of the squares, leaving a ½in (12mm) seam allowance. As you stitch across each of the folded edges of the rectangles, reverse stitch for strength.

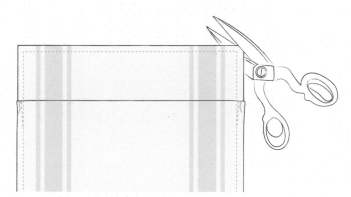

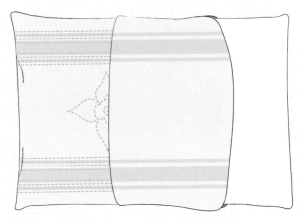

7 Cut diagonally across each corner, being careful not to snip your stitches.

8 Turn your cushion cover the right way out and tease out the corners (pushing with a knitting needle from the inside helps). Gently wash by hand if pencil lines show, then iron. Slide your cushion pad inside the inner sleeve before covering with the outer sleeve.

MACHINE QUILTING USING APPLIQUÉ

QUILTING ON A MACHINE CAN SIMPLY BE ROWS OF PARALLEL STITCHES OR IT CAN BE COMPLEX PATTERNS OF FREE-FORM STITCHING. HERE IS AN INTRODUCTION TO HOW TO USE MACHINE QUILTING TO DO MORE THAN JUST SECURE THE THREE LAYERS OF MATERIAL TOGETHER.

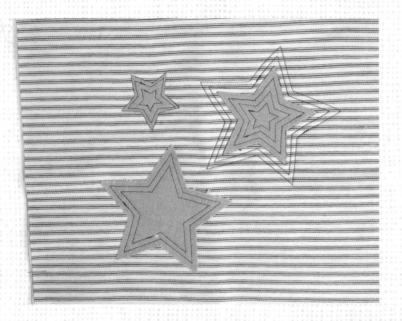

So here is a method, which is a step towards Free-form machine quilting, using Appliqué. Appliqué is when shapes of contrasting fabrics are used to decorate a quilt top before quilting the layers together and zigzag stitch is used to bind the raw edges or sometimes the edges are turned under and slip stitched. I have adapted the technique and here the appliqué shapes are used as guidelines to quilt the three layers of the sandwich together. This way, a stitch pattern can be built up whilse still having something to follow. Use contrasting thread to emphasis the quilting pattern.

For some quilters, the process they enjoy most is patchworking and quilting is just what you have to do after you have made your quilt top. For others, the process of machine quilting is what draws them in. Advanced quilters use free-form quilting to produce intricate patterns across the whole surface of their quilt tops. The technique is achieved by dropping the feed dogs (the gripping plates that feed the material under the needle) and guiding the fabric by hand. Doing this enables control of the direction of the stitching and the length of each stitch. Free-form stitching is akin to rubbing your stomach and patting your head at the same time. A novice quilter has enough on their hands without having to control the direction and length of each stitch.

Tip Iron-on transfer adhesive comes in various different strengths. If your shapes are cut from a thick fabric, use the strongest strength to ensure your appliqué sticks to the base fabric.

1 Using a pencil, trace a small design onto the smooth side of your iron-on transfer adhesive, then cut it out about ⅛in (2mm) from your pencil line. Using a hot iron with no steam – and making sure the rough side of the transfer adhesive is facing the fabric – press it onto the wrong side of your fabric.

Tip When you are attaching the appliqué shapes, first run the iron over the background fabric to warm it up. This will help the iron-on transfer adhesive adhere better to the fabric.

2 Cut out your design, following the pencil line exactly, then peel off the backing paper. You will see that a layer of adhesive has been left on the fabric.

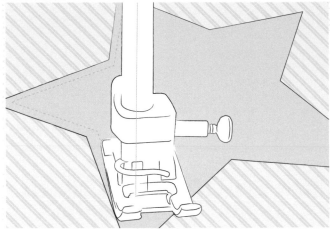

3 Place your design onto your quilt top and iron into position. Make absolutely sure the glue side is facing the fabric and not the iron! Press down gently rather than move the iron across the design – this will avoid distorting the fabric. Now make your quilt top into a quilt sandwich (see page 26).

4 Referring back to machine stitch basics (see page 22), stitch around the edge of the motif, securing it to the quilt top, batting and backing fabric. As you stitch, keep the right-hand edge of the sewing machine foot in line with the motif edge. Refer to page 23 for how to turn a corner.

5 After you have stitched around the motif, overlap slightly and reverse stitch to secure.

6 Move the foot so that the right-hand edge lines up with the line of stitching that you have just made. Run a new line of stitches around the motif, parallel to the first.

7 Depending on the project you are working on and how dense you want your stitching to be, you can echo the shape of the motif with lines of stitching on the background fabric.

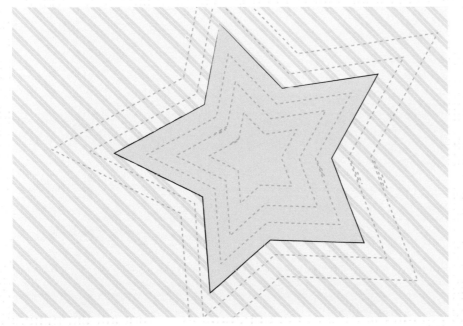

Project nine

TABLE RUNNER

QUILTING IN CONTINUOUS, FLOWING LINES ALONG THE LENGTH OF THE FABRIC, THIS MODERN
DESIGN INCORPORATES A SIMPLE LEAF SHAPE, DISPLAYING YOUR MACHINE QUILTING SKILLS
WITHOUT DISTRACTION FROM ANY PATCHWORK.

YOU WILL NEED

- 14 x 50in (36 x 127cm) linen or cotton
- 16 x 52in (41 x 132cm) cotton or linen
  backing fabric
- 150in (380cm) of 4in (10cm) binding
  strips in same fabric as backing fabric
- Fabric scraps in three contrasting colours
- 16 x 52in (41 x 132cm) cotton batting
- Contrasting and matching general-
  purpose thread
- Dressmaking, paper and small
  needlework scissors
- Machine quilting needle (size 90/14)
- No.9 sharp or embroidery needle
- Quilting or dressmaking pins
- Thimble
- Seam ripper
- Tape measure
- Pencil
- Air-fade pen
- Tracing paper
- 24in (60cm) iron-on transfer adhesive
- Leaf template (see page 115)

FINISHED SIZE

13 x 49in (33 x 125cm)

TECHNIQUES USED

Machine quilting using appliqué
(see page 98)
Preparing the quilt sandwich
(see page 26)
Tacking (see page 20)
Starting and finishing a machine stitch
(see page 22)
Turning a corner (see page 23)
Squaring up (see page 25)
Binding edges (see page 28)

MATERIALS TO USE

For this project it is important to choose
a fabric that is quite stiff and will not
stretch at all, such as a close-weave linen
or cotton. This is because the lines of
stitching along the length of the table
runner can cause the fabric to move
slightly and wrinkle. A stiff fabric will be
easier to keep in place. The scraps can
be a different type of fabric from the
quilt top but again, choose fabrics that
are quite stiff.

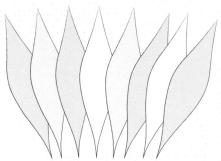

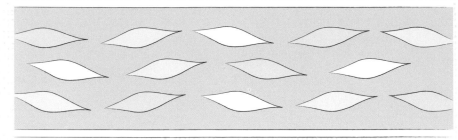

1 Using the leaf template and following steps 1 and 2 on page 99, trace 15 leaves onto your iron-on adhesive and adhere them to three contrasting fabrics (five of each). Cut them out and remove the backing.

2 Place your background fabric onto a flat surface, with a towel or thick cloth underneath. Arrange your leaves on the fabric, as shown, aiming for alternating lines of leaves, with a regular space between each one. Make sure the bottom of each leaf marked on your template faces in the same direction. Carefully iron the leaves in place.

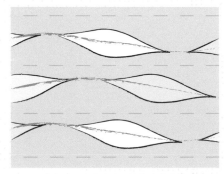

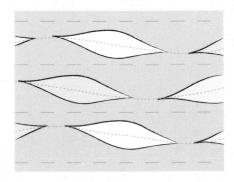

3 Referring to step 3 on page 100, and using your appliquéd leaf fabric as a quilt top, prepare your quilt sandwich. As the table runner is narrow, it is only necessary to tack along the length of the quilt sandwich, as shown.

4 Using an air-fade pen (or a pencil, but wash out any marks when complete), draw a line from end to end along each of the three rows of leaves, running through each leaf's centre. As your leaves are not in a straight line, your line will naturally curve.

5 Going from end to end, stitch along your pen lines, starting with the central row of leaves and then the two outer rows. Go slowly and use your hands to guide the fabric through the machine. For a stronger effect, use contrasting thread.

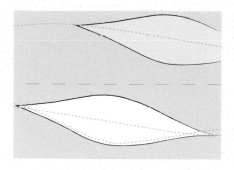

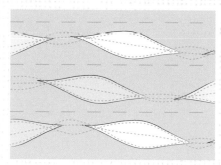

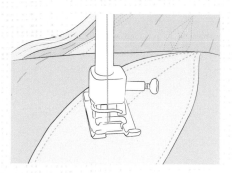

6 To sew around each leaf, start at one end and follow your existing stitch lines. When you come to each leaf, stitch along one side of the leaf instead of going through the centre. Try to keep these lines wavy, as wobbles add to the design.

7 The next line of stitches needs to go around the other side of each leaf. Note how the stitched lines do not follow the leaves exactly, but form a loop between each leaf.

8 To add the veins of the leaves, you need to stitch once more along the central line of stitches, starting from the top (thinner) end of the leaves. Halfway down the first leaf, stop when the needle is down through the material. Swivel the fabric about 45 degrees, reverse stitch for 1in (2.5cm), then release and stitch forwards, back to the central line of stitches – stop with needle down.

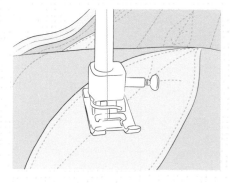

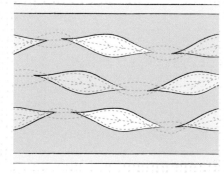

9 Next swivel the fabric in the opposite direction and repeat step 8 to form a 'V' shape. Continue down the row of leaves, adding two 'Vs' to each leaf.

10 Square up your quilt sandwich and bind the edges, using the same fabric as your backing fabric. Remove your quilting tacking stitches and iron your project.

MITRED CORNER

THIS TECHNIQUE IS ALL ABOUT ATTENTION TO DETAIL. WHEN YOU HAVE SPENT TIME MAKING A QUILT, IT IS A NICE TOUCH TO FINISH OFF THE BINDING WITH THESE MITRED CORNERS, WHICH REDUCE BULK AND MAKE YOUR FINISHED PROJECT LOOK EVEN MORE NEAT AND TIDY.

A mitred corner is a particular kind of joint. When two sides meet at a right angle, a mitred joint will run from the outside corner to the inside corner, forming a 45-degree angle and a nice neat line. In sewing terms, this means that when you are binding and want to turn a right-angled corner, it is possible to do so without cutting the binding strip or binding each side separately. There is far less bulk at each corner when you do it this way and the ends of the binding strips can be placed along the sides of the quilt in a less conspicuous place.

It is trickier than the basic folding over technique for binding, which is why it is the last technique in the book, but if you have got this far into your quilting journey and if you intend to complete the last project, it is worth getting to grips with this technique. When you come to hem the binding, as with the folding over technique, this can be done either by hand or carefully on the machine. Personally, I like to hem my binding by hand, as I do not like the line of the machine stitching right around a quilt. To a new sewer, it can be quite daunting to hand stitch the binding on a full-size quilt, but trust me, it never takes as long as it looks like it's going to and it is an excuse to sit down and take it easy after completing a big project.

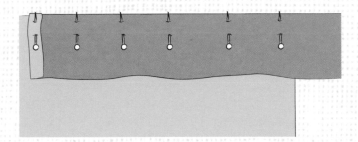

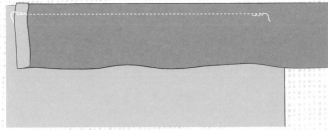

1 Fold over the end of your first binding strip by about 1in (2.5cm). Then, starting about one-third along one of the longest edges of the quilt and with the folded edge facing upwards, place the binding strip along the edge of the quilt sandwich, RST. Pin for machine stitch (see page 19), but only up to the first corner.

2 Using a ½in (12mm) seam allowance, stitch along this first edge, stopping ½in (12mm) from the corner. Reverse stitch to secure.

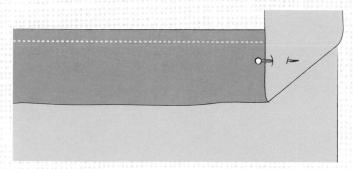

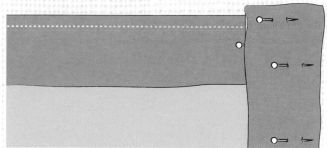

3 Remove from the machine and place on a flat surface. Fold the binding strip upwards so it forms a continuous straight line with the next side and is at a right angle with the side already stitched. A small diagonal fold will form at the corner. Secure this with a pin.

4 Fold the binding strip back down and pin down the next side. When you reach the next corner repeat steps 1–4. Do this at all four corners. Finally, pin and stitch along the first edge until you are back where you started. Overlap the strips by 2in (5cm) so no raw edges are exposed.

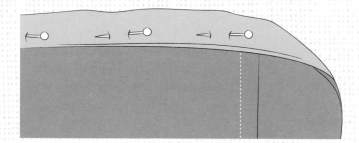

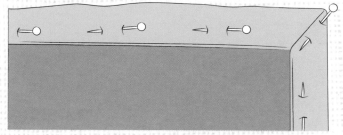

5 Next turn your quilt over, fold the binding strip over by ½in (12mm) and then fold again so the folded edge sits alongside the seam just sewn. Pin right up to each corner, which will naturally fold at a 45-degree angle.

6 Next, fold and pin the binding along the adjacent edge – the 45-degree fold will run from the outside edge through to the inside – forming the mitred corner. Continue around until all the binding is pinned. Use hemming stitch (see page 21) to finish. Run a couple of extra stitches up each mitred corner to secure or carefully machine stitch. Finally, press the seams.

Tip When you are sewing towards each corner, exactly where you stop the stitching will depend on your seam allowance. When sewing with a ½in (12mm) seam allowance, you must stop ½in (12mm) before the edge. If using a ¼in (6mm) you would stop ¼in (6mm) before the edge, etc.

BED COVER

ALTHOUGH BIG, THIS QUILT IS MADE FROM A MIXTURE OF SOLID FABRIC SQUARES AND SIMPLE QUILT BLOCKS, SO IT BUILDS UP QUICKLY. INCORPORATING MANY OF THE TECHNIQUES DEMONSTRATED IN THIS BOOK, IT WILL GIVE YOU THE CHANCE TO PRACTISE ALL YOU KNOW.

YOU WILL NEED

- About 5½ sq yards/metres of at least ten different fabrics (see Materials to Use on the right)
- 177in (4.5m) from 59in (150cm) width cotton or linen fabric (backing/binding)
- 80in (200cm) from 96in (244cm) width cotton batting
- Matching general-purpose thread
- Dressmaking, paper and small needlework scissors
- Machine universal needle (size 90/14)
- Machine quilting needle (size 90/14)
- No.9 sharp or embroidery needle
- Quilting and dressmaking pins
- Thimble
- Seam ripper
- Tape measure
- Craft knife, steel ruler and cutting mat
- Pencil and paper

FINISHED SIZE

96 x 72in (240 x 180cm)

TECHNIQUES USED

Strip patchwork (see page 56)

Squaring up (see page 25)

Simple quilt block (see page 64)

Pin for machine stitch (see page 19)

Preparing the quilt sandwich (see page 26)

Tacking (see page 20)

Stitch in the Ditch (see page 27)

Reverse stitching (see page 22)

Binding edges (see page 28)

Mitred corner (see page 106)

MATERIALS TO USE

See pages 14–15 to help you choose at least ten suitable prints and patterns for your quilt top. If buying fabric, then 10 x 26in (66cm) from a 45in (115cm) width fabric of each will give you plenty – using scraps from other projects will mean you need to buy less. Use the same fabric for the binding and backing and for nice long binding strips follow step 8 for cutting the binding.

CUTTING OUT FABRIC

You will need to cut three paper templates: one 13in (33cm) square, one 5in (13cm square and a 13in (33cm) x 5in (13cm) strip. Using the first template, cut out 18 squares that are 13 x 13in (33 x 33cm) – one from each fabric and eight from a random selection. Now cut 54 strips of fabric using the 13in (33cm) x 5in (13cm) strip template, cutting five of each of your ten fabrics and four from a random selection. With the 5in (13cm) square template, cut 108 squares of fabric that are 5 x 5in (13 x 13cm), cutting ten of each of your ten fabrics and eight from a random selection.

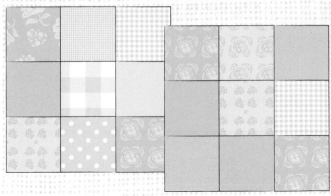

1 Follow the instructions for the Strip patchwork technique to make strips up into 18 quilt blocks, 13 x 13in (33 x 33cm). Try to make each block a different combination of fabrics. Iron all seams in one direction, then square up each quilt block by checking it against the paper template.

2 Following the Simple quilt block technique instructions, and using the 5in (13cm) squares, make 12 Nine Patch quilt blocks that are 13 x 13in (33 x 33in). Again, use a variety of different fabrics within each block and square up each quilt block by checking it against the paper template.

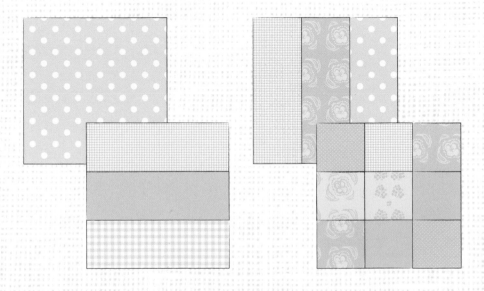

3 You now have the 48 basic blocks needed to construct the quilt: 18 solid fabric blocks, 12 Nine Patch blocks and 18 Strip blocks – think of the Strip blocks as nine horizontal Strip blocks and nine vertical Strip blocks.

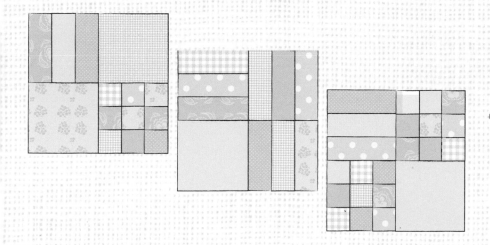

4 Assemble these basic blocks into larger blocks of four. On a flat surface, usually the floor, take a random selection of 12 basic blocks and arrange to form three larger blocks of four. Pin for machine stitch.

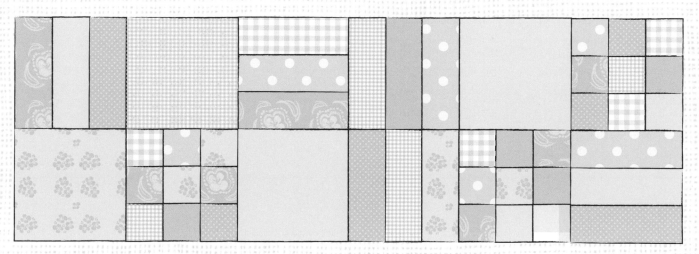

5 In the same way as you would sew smaller blocks together, sew these three larger blocks together to form a strip, then repeat steps 4 and 5 with the remaining basic quilt blocks to form four strips, each made up of 12 basic blocks.

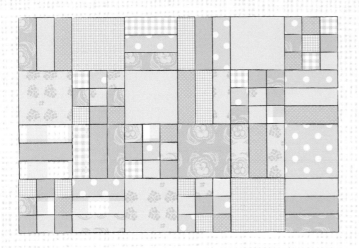

6 Take two of these strips and, with RST and matching seams where possible, pin for machine stitch and sew together. Repeat this step with the other two strips to form two large sections.

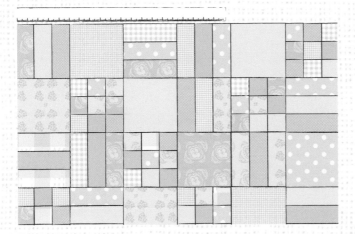

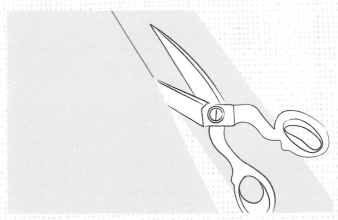

7 Again, with RST, and matching seams where possible, sew these two large sections of blocks together. Square up your quilt top, remembering to measure from the centre of the quilt top outwards, so you don't cut too much from either side.

8 Prepare your backing fabric and binding strips. First, cut a 3in (8cm) strip from each side of your fabric, cutting a continuous length parallel to the selvedge along the whole of the 177in (4.5m) edge. These will be your binding strips.

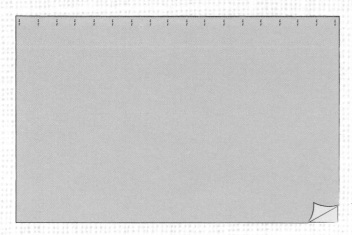

9 From the remaining fabric, cut two lengths of 79in (200cm). Place these rectangles RST and pin for machine stitch along one of the longer 79in (200cm) sides. Sew together to form the size of backing fabric needed for the quilt. Iron the seam open.

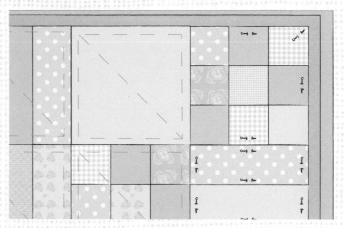

10 Prepare your quilt sandwich. Spend time on this stage – smooth out wrinkles and tack close to the seams of each block to make sure the layers don't move while quilting.

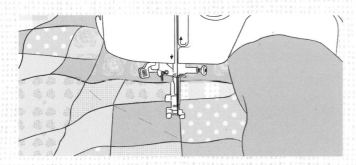

11 To quilt this bed cover, refer to the Stitch in the Ditch method and stitch in the seams of each basic block; work across the quilt and then along the length. To quilt the basic blocks into smaller sections, follow the seams of the Nine Patch blocks and the Strip blocks to divide into smaller sections. Reverse stitch at the beginning and end of stitching to secure.

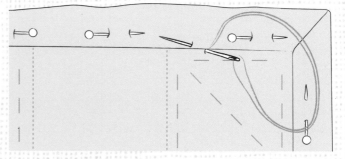

12 Trim off the excess batting and backing fabric and bind the edges to complete your quilt. Use the 3in (8cm) strips to create a final binding width of 1in (2.5cm). Follow the mitred corners technique for a nice neat finish. All that is left to do is remove the tacking stitches and iron out any wrinkles.

Templates

Copy at 100% size.

lavender keepsake

cushion

table runner

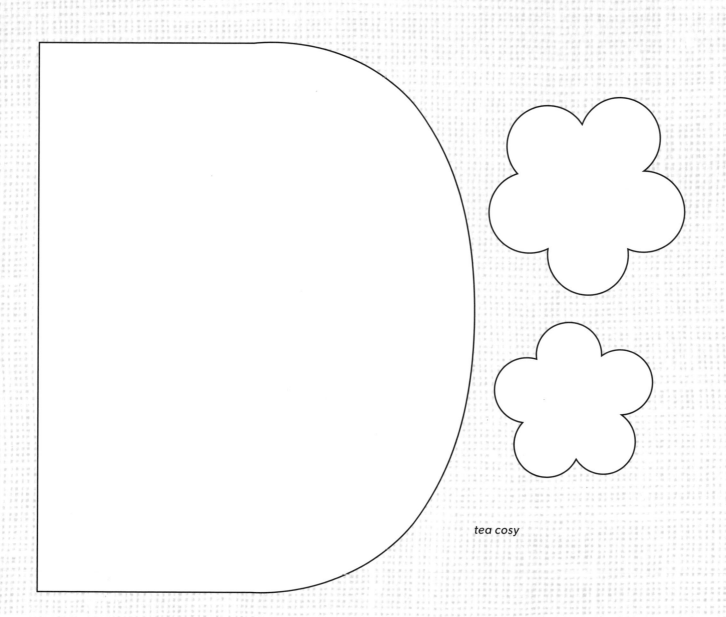

tea cosy

Resources

UK

Doughty's Patchwork and Quilting
5 Capuchin Yard
Off Church Street
Hereford
HR1 2LR
+44 01432 267542
www.doughtysonline.co.uk

European Quilting Supplies Ltd
11 Iliffe House,
Iliffe Avenue,
Leicester
LE2 5LS
+44 0116 271 0033
www.eqsuk.com

The Cotton Patch
1285 Stratford Road
Hall Green
Birmingham
B28 9AJ
+44 0121 702 2840
www.cottonpatch.co.uk

Calico Laine
16 Liscard Crescent
Wallasey
Wirral
CH44 1AE
+44 0151 336 3939
www.calicolaine.co.uk

The Patchwork Dog & Basket
The Needlemakers
West Street
Lewes
East Sussex
BN7 2NZ
+44 01273 483886
www.patchworkdogandbasket.co.uk

US

Patchwork Plus, Inc.
17 Killdeer Lane
Dayton
Virginia
22821
Toll Free +1 877-674-4821
www.patchworkplus-quilting.com

Fat Quarter Shop
PO Box 1544
Manchaca
TX 78652
Toll Free +1 866-826-2069
www.fatquartershop.com

Quilting Warehouse
9019 Soquel Dr.
Aptos
CA 95003
+1 831-768-4200
www.quilting-warehouse.com

About the author

Rachel Clare Reynolds has been an artist, craftsperson and teacher for over 25 years. During this time, she has worked in metal, concrete and ceramics before returning to her first love – textiles. Her textiles work explores how traditional embroidery and quilting techniques can be reinterpreted in a contemporary way. Rachel is passionate about keeping traditional craft skills alive.

Acknowledgements

I would like to thank my Grandmother, Dorothy Whiting, for teaching my mum how to sew, and then thank my mum, Brenda Reynolds, for teaching me. Without them I would not have written this book, I would be needing to read it.

I would also like to thank one very special sewing queen, who let me raid her scrap bag week after week and pick out all the most gorgeous fabrics – without Teri Dawkins this book would not be so lovely.

Last but by no means least, I need to say thank you to my husband Mash and children, Lily, Toby and Gabriel for being impressed by me writing this book.

GMC Publications would like to thank:

The Patchwork Dog & Basket in Lewes for the kind loan of quilting materials and equipment; Christian and Rhoda Funnell for allowing us to photograph at the Old Forge in South Heighton, East Sussex (www.christianfunnell.com); and Amelia Holmwood for photographic styling.

Index

To order a book, or to request
a catalogue, contact:

GMC Publications Ltd
Castle Place, 166 High Street,
Lewes, East Sussex,
BN7 1XU
United Kingdom
Tel: +44 (0)1273 488005
www.gmcbooks.com